PROFILES *of*
FAITH AND PRAISE

TESTIMONIES BY OVERCOMERS

COMPILED BY
EUGENE NEVILLE

Extreme Overflow Publishing
Dacula, GA
USA

Extreme Overflow Publishing
Dacula, GA
USA

Extreme Overflow Publishing
A Brand of Extreme Overflow Enterprises, Inc
P.O. Box 1811
Dacula, GA 30019

www.extremeoverflow.com
Send feedback to info@extreme-overflow-enterprises.com
Cover Artwork by Ruth Neville

Printed in the United States of America

Library of Congress Catalogin-Publication 2019917754
Data is available for this title. ISBN: 978-1-7340638-2-0

PROFILES *of*
FAITH AND PRAISE

Compiled by
EUGENE NEVILLE

If I can help somebody, as I pass along
If I can cheer somebody with a word or song
If I can show somebody how they're
    traveling wrong
Then my living shall not be in vain.
If I can do my duty as a good man ought
If I can bring back beauty to a world
    up wrought
If I can spread love's message as the
    Master taught
Then my living shall not be in vain.

by Alma Bazel

Table of Contents

MAY GOD CONTINUE TO
ENCOURAGE AND bless you
AS You READ EACH of these
POWERful Testimonies of
BEAUTIFUL OVER Comers.
SUCH AS Yourself.

Rev. Eugene L. Noble
~ 2019 ~

Introduction

God shall wipe away all tears from their eyes;
and there shall be no more death,
neither sorrow, crying, neither shall there be
any more pain: for the former things
have passed away

Revelation 21:4

God always hears the faintest cries from His children and delights to rescue them from all their troubles and sin. In these readings are the honest questions and answered prayer requests of 14 people from around the country who willingly shared their testimonies, how God delivered, healed, and transformed their lives, amidst their most painful and life-altering experiences.

My prayer is that you will be encouraged by these testimonies, so that no matter what difficult or painful challenges you may experience; nevertheless, by faith, you will continue to hold onto God's unchanging hand, knowing that God understands and has already provided everything to see you through the tests and lead you to your anointed destiny.

What God was delighted to do in others, believe in your heart that He is willing to do for you. These facts shall always be true. God is the only one who can change the miserable conditions in our lives into the mysterious. The mysterious, unanswerable questions into the marvelous blessings. The marvelous blessings into the majestic glory of God. Whereby, we will be ushered into the holy presence of Almighty God. In the presence of Almighty God, we shall find deliverance from all our sins. We shall find peace that surpasses all human understanding. We shall find direction for each of our footsteps as we walk on the path of righteousness. We shall find new strength as we yield to the Holy Spirit. In addition, we shall behold the Lord Jesus Christ in all His glory. We shall live eternally in heaven.

Rev. Eugene L. Neville

Testimony of
Cyndy Newell Bell
North Carolina
**Don't Forget All of the Things God Has
Done Over the Years**

Remember how the Lord your God led you
all the way in the wilderness these 40 years,
to humble and test you in order to know
what was in your heart, whether or not you would
keep his commands, He humbled you,
causing you to hunger and then, feeding you
with manna, which neither you nor your ancestors
had known, to teach you that man does not live on
bread alone but on every word that
contest from the mouth of the Lord.

Deuteronomy 8:2-3

My life growing up was simple; naïve, even. I was the oldest of four children born over the span of a little more than four years. My mom was a former schoolteacher and kept us very close to home. My dad worked at the grain mill and was always home at the same time; just as dinner was going on the table. Our Saturdays meant loading up the station wagon and driving 30 miles up the road to my grandpa's farm, arriving just in time for the mid-day meal. This was the highlight of my week as I loved the farm, whether it meant helping with haying in the summer or sugaring in the spring, or just being there on the hill enjoying the peace and quiet.

When I was 13, we moved from town to a small village and a two-room schoolhouse. I was the new girl in town and ignored, at least by the other girls. My life consisted of schoolwork and escaping into books. Even when I got into high school, the only difference was now I was also working at whatever jobs were available. I was a loner; smart, but socially inept. College was a struggle as I sought to find my path in life. I had ideas of being a doctor or a teacher, but my lack of confidence stymied me. I majored in Bible, then education, and finally thought I'd found my niche in psychology. My senior year of school, I met someone I thought was the answer to my search for love. We married shortly after my graduation and set off on our big adventure.

Eighteen years and five children later, he woke up one morning, packed his bags, and walked out of my life. His parting comment was, "I never really loved you. I just thought I could fix you." In hindsight, I believe it was as much about filling his emptiness, his "black hole," as it was about me. I have always dealt with depression to some degree. I had hit rock bottom once in my marriage, only this time it was accompanied by severe anxiety. I had gone back to school and was about half-way through the first year of a two-year nursing program. I could not continue and still maintain some semblance of parenting. I did not know how I was going to cope with five children between the ages of three and 11, but God was there. He reminded me that vengeance was His, and that I was to just let go and let Him take care of things. Even when my daughter would rage against me and say it was all my fault, He gave me the grace to keep my peace. One of my keepsakes is the Father's Day card she gave me when she was about 16. She wrote "Happy Father's Day to the best father I ever had."

Through all those years, God was faithful. He met our needs and gave me the strength to find my footing. I regrouped and went back to school, this time taking classes in computer programming. There were times a check would come in the mail with a note "Thought you could use this" or "I meant to send this sooner ... I'm so sorry." But the beauty was that they always came at a time when they were needed most.

When my two oldest kids ran away and ended up

half-way across the country, I went into full panic mode. As I lay in bed, trying to sleep, God reminded me that He knew exactly where they were, and He was far more capable of caring for them than I was. Do I feel that I failed as a mother? In so many ways, yes. Did I love my kids and try to make sure they knew I loved them? To the best I knew how, yes. Do I still feel like I've failed them? Yes. Have they succeeded in life in spite of it? For the most part, yes.

I remember some of the struggles. The winter night the fuel ran out, and I loaded the kids up in the van, grabbed the 5-gallon gas can, and went to the gas station to get kerosene because someone said you could burn it in place of #2 fuel oil. Coming home and climbing up on a kitchen chair balanced on the icy ground, pouring kerosene into the oil tank and spilling it all down the front of my jacket. Going back for more until we had enough to get through the night. Or the night when they were little that the heat went out during a snowstorm. I've got four sick kids who have been throwing up and a nursing baby. The landlord can't make it into town until morning, so we're sleeping on mattresses in the kitchen in front of the oven to keep warm, while their dad is snoozing away in the bedroom. I learned early on that if I wanted to go anywhere or do anything, I had to learn to do it alone. So, I would load up the kids in the old VW van, and we would head for "home," which was 12 hours away. Kids who would have killed each other driving across town were perfect angels on these long road trips. Some of our best memories are the trips to Vermont to see Grandpa; or the trip to Tallahassee, where they learned to throw nets into the Gulf to catch shrimp and crabs.

To tell that story, I need to back up a bit. When my husband moved out, we were living in a small house. The kids were getting bigger. Four boys who are now well over six-feet tall and very active; and one girl who needed her own space. I knew I needed to find a bigger place. One Sunday, I felt led to pick up a newspaper and search out the For Rent ads. And there it was. Three bedrooms upstairs for the boys, a bedroom suite downstairs for my daughter, and a dining room that I converted into my bedroom on the middle level.

So back to that trip to Florida. It came about after I decided to have a yard sale. Things were going well, but toward the end of the day, I sent out a quick prayer; Lord, I really need to sell this-and-this and that. An odd bunch of unrelated items, including some old wire fencing. A few minutes later, a lady drove up in her old pickup truck, looked around and said, "I'll take this and this and that" – the very things I'd just prayed about! Learning to listen to that "still, small voice" has worked for me. When He is in control, and the timing is His, things often go wonderfully smooth. Does He always give us that supernatural peace? No, but maybe that's so that we will look back at our lives and remember the many ways He has led us through the wildernesses. I still deal with depression and discouragement, but I know that He is there and still loves and cares for me.

And now I face a new struggle, a new challenge. Once again, I am at a crossroads where I do not know the outcome. I spent about 13 years as a single parent before remarrying 15 years ago. Working full time and watching my children navigate the gulf between childhood and adulthood. They each carry some baggage from those days, but I am proud to say that for the most part, they are successful. For me, these last 15 years were a time of maturing and putting into practice things I learned along the way.

None of the things that happen in our lives are wasted. God uses them to prepare us for the next phase of our lives. This has been a time of growing in patience, beyond what I sometimes thought I was capable of, as I experience what living with someone with PTSD is like. It is also a time of new fears and anxieties as I grow older and face the challenges of aging, as well as the probability of being alone again soon. And here's where I remind myself to look back and remember. Remember those hard times when I wasn't sure how I was going to make it, but He always came through. I remain steadfast in knowing that the One I trust will be with me wherever I go, whatever the challenge. Do I have moments when my eyes leak a little? Yes. Do I know what the outcome will be? No. Am I going forward cautiously, listening for that guiding nudge? I hope so. I may be alone again soon. It won't be because it's what I want. But I'm also learning that we can't hold on to things that aren't meant to be. And I know wherever I end up, He will never ever forsake me.

Testimony of
Cynthia Allen
Florida
Try To Understand

Honor thy father and thy mother;
that thy days may be long upon the land
which the Lord thy God giveth thee.

Exodus 20: 12

This is the first commandment with a promise.

I look back over my life and realize that I have truly been blessed. I give total praise and honor to my Heavenly Father and my earthly parents for their many sacrifices. As children, the first thing we learn at home and at Sunday school is the 10 Commandments. My parents made sure we understood the words, "Honor thy father and thy mother." We showed honor by our actions and attitudes. We learned to obey, to be respectful, and do as we were told. There were no if-or-buts about it. Our parents were very strict and did not play! What they said, they meant. You didn't question them, and they didn't repeat themselves. Whenever something went wrong in the house, my father would line all the children up to find out who the guilty party was. If no one admitted to the wrongdoing, everyone got a spanking.

In relation to our father, we honored and obeyed him out of fear. It was not until we became older that we realized that most of their corrective measures were for our good. In retrospect, they were attempting to teach us valuable life principles.

How to follow instructions.

How to use wisdom.

How to discern right from wrong.

How to act responsibly.

How to respect your elders and other people.

The values of kindness, honesty, compassion, generosity, etc.

Their goal was that we all grow up to be honest and decent human beings.

From The Projects To Our Palace

I was born in Charleston, South Carolina. My father was a carpenter by trade; my mother worked as a house cleaner for a white family. This was life in the 1950s. My father was a grown man; however, he was never called by his name. He was only addressed as "boy." He joined the Army during World War II. He went to Germany, England, and France. When he returned home to Charleston, he was still "boy." He told me later in life that no matter how old he was, if he stayed in South Carolina he would always be "boy." When I was nine, my father made the decision to move the entire family north to a place called Jersey City, New Jersey. This move changed the future for our entire family.

We moved from the projects of Charleston to a cold-water flat in Jersey City. The apartment building had a coal stove in the kitchen and a kerosene stove in the living room. We had three bedrooms and one bathroom for 10 people.

Today, my husband and I are blessed to live in a 5-bedroom home with five full-baths and two half-baths, which we gladly share with family and friends on holidays and any time they choose to visit.

From Chicken Necks, Gizzards, And Livers To A Whole Chicken

I was the third child in a family which consisted of five girls and three boys. We grew up poor; however, we did not realize we were poor until we left our neighborhood or went to school. There were plenty of days that we didn't have food to eat. Being from South Carolina, we lived off the state staple, which was rice. For dinner, we had:

Rice, pork, and beans,

Rice and cow peas,

Rice and black eye peas,

Rice and black beans,

Rice and kidney beans,

Rice and lima beans,

Rice and northern beans,

Rice and pinto beans,

Rice and navy beans,

Rice and butter beans,

Rice and every bean or peas imaginable,

Rice and butter,

Rice and gravy,

Red rice, yellow rice, rice and more rice.

I don't eat rice today because of the amount of rice I ate growing up.

My mother was a magnificent cook, and I always looked forward to Sunday dinners. After church, we would come home to a feast, which would consist of fried chicken, yams, potato salad, collard greens, and red Kool-Aid. One chicken would feed a family of 10. Everyone would get one piece of chicken, and someone would always get the neck, gizzard, and liver. Today, my husband and I are blessed to be able to grill a whole chicken, and no one must eat the neck, gizzard, or liver unless they want to.

If it were not rice for dinner it would be potatoes,

> French-fried potatoes,
>
> Hash brown potatoes,
>
> Baked potatoes,
>
> Mashed potatoes,
>
> Sweet potatoes,
>
> Home-fried potatoes,
>
> Au Gratin Potatoes,

Baked, broiled, fried, roasted, or boiled; it didn't

matter, Mama could work her magic, and I love potatoes.

I Knew You Loved Us Even Though You Never Said It

My father only had a fourth-grade education; however, you would never know it. He had life experience smarts. He was tall, handsome, funny, and quick- witted. With his carpentry skills, he could build anything. My father loved to sing and dance. In church, he sang in the male choir, Gospel choir, and senior choir. Daddy also loved to play the card game bid whist and drink vodka. Daddy claims that vodka cures all ailments.

Because dad did not finish school, education for us was very important to him. Our job, according to dad, was to go to school and get good grades. It didn't matter that neither he nor mom would be able help us if we had problems with a school assignment. According to dad, that was not his problem; he did not ask us to come to his job and help him when he had a problem. He would not accept a grade lower than a B. Neither he nor mom would ever attend a parent-teachers meeting, and we were threatened with death if they ever had to take a day off from work because we did something bad at school.

My mother graduated from grammar school and

completed the 10th grade. At the age of 58, she went to night school and earned her high school diploma. She worked at a large laundry that washed and pressed hospital linen. Every day, she would come home with burns on her arms and hands.

While our parents were very hard workers, there simply was never enough money to feed and clothe eight children. There were always arguments over money. Mama was constantly telling Daddy:

The children need food,

The children need shoes,

The children need clothes,

The children need everything,

The rent is due,

The car payment is due,

The insurance is due,

The electric bill is due.

Something was always due, and there was never enough money to pay for anything.

We rarely went to a doctor, and if the ailment couldn't be cured with rock candy and castor oil or Scott Emulsion cod liver oil, it just wasn't going to be fixed. I had very poor eyesight in school and had to sit on the front row because my parents couldn't afford to get me glasses. It wasn't until I was 15 that I finally got a pair of glasses.

Our parents were wonderful people; my father would give you the shirt of his back and was available to help anyone at any time. The one thing I will always remember about my mother was that she never ate until all the children were finished. Then she would eat whatever scraps we left on our plates. Mama sacrificed so that we could eat. She did what a mother does, and there was no doubt in my mind that she would have given her life for us if she had to. My mother was committed to family; even though we had nothing, everyone was always welcome. If you needed a place to stay, you could always stay with us.

We're Moving On Up

Because my father was in the Army, he was able to get a VA loan that enabled him to buy a home. We were finally doing The Jeffersons; we were moving on up to a two-family house on the corner of Bergen and Virginia Avenue in Jersey City. We had finally arrived. We still had three bedrooms and one bath, but it was ours.

Correction, it belonged to our parents and the bank. As time went by, things really began to get better. The blood sucking children who needed food, clothing, shoes, rock candy, castor oil, and cod liver oil began to get older. We graduated from high school and were finally able to contribute to the household expenses. Because, as my father put it, "no one lives for free," and we were going to pay him back for all the money we cost him.

In the late 60s, with only high school diplomas, my older sister and I went to New York's financial district. She got a job with the federal government and was able to retire with 40 years of service. I got a job with the Bell System, which consisted of AT&T, Western Electric, and the local telephone company. I retired after 35 years of service.

My older brother joined the Air Force after high school. After retiring from the military, he got another good job and was able to retire from that as well.

My younger sister got a job with the Post Office. Another sister, an insurance company. The youngest sister joined the Navy.

The best thing about the move to Bergen Avenue was that I met the love of my life. The cutest, best-looking person I have never known. Well, maybe he wasn't the best looking because I did need glasses, and they do say love is blind. Nonetheless, 53 years later and after 47 years of marriage, he still looks good to me.

The Rise And Fall Of The Family

I never saw my parents show any signs of affection toward each other. I never heard my dad tell my mom he loved her. I never heard my mom tell my dad she loved him. They never told us children they loved us. However, we knew they loved us. Everything they did said they loved us; every beating we were sad they loved us; every punishment received said they loved us. They just didn't know how to say the words. They did the best they could with what they had, and now that we're older, we understand. Unfortunately, our parent's relationship, or lack of relationship, suffered during the lean times, and there was no coming back.

I'm Going Home

Thirty-one years earlier, we left South Carolina as a family. At the age of 65, mama decided she was going home. Home was Wando, South Carolina, where she grew up as a child. The return trip, however, did not include daddy. Our grandmother had five children and left each child an acre of land. Mama was going home to friends who never left. Mama was going home to peace and quiet, away from the noise, chaos, and busy life of inner city living. Mama was going home to country living, trees, woods, and dirt roads. Mama was going home without daddy.

Happiness And Sadness

Mama was happy; she was home. Mama worked hard all her life; however, none of her jobs provided a pension, and her monthly Social Security benefits were only $500 per month. All our lives mama told us children to put aside money for a rainy day, don't spend so much, buy what you need and not what you want. Mama practiced what she preached and as a result was able to buy a doublewide trailer for her acre of land. Mama lived on $500 per month, and her children gladly made sure that she was able to finally get the things she deserved, not just needed.

Daddy was sad; he could not believe mama would leave him, even though our entire lives mama always said she would return home someday. As I mentioned earlier, daddy loved to sing, dance, play cards, and drink vodka. What I didn't say was daddy also loved the women, and the women loved him. Once mama left town, the women also left. They didn't want to be bothered with him. Daddy's pension and Social Security benefits were four times what mama made; however, he was not able to accomplish what she did.

In 2008, while visiting dad in Jersey City, I called my mom and siblings to inform them of the condition daddy was in. We agreed that the house would be sold, and dad would live with me in Florida until a family home was built in Wando, South Carolina.

Your Father Is No Longer Welcome Here

Daddy came to live with us at the age of 84; he had dementia and was living in his own world. Not the world where he was 84 years old, but the world in which he thought he was in his 40s. As retirees, my husband and I were content to stay home and enjoy doing nothing. My father, however, wanted to go out all the time. He wanted to go dancing, he wanted to go to a party, he just wanted to go out and have fun. To keep him happy, I found a nice senior center to take him to. The center provided lunch, and a nice place for the seniors to enjoy each other's company while playing cards, dominos, reading papers, and magazines. Well, that was the intent of the center before my father arrived.

When I brought my father to the center, there was about 20 women and 8 men. My father became the rooster in the hen house. My father loved women, and addressed the women as honey, baby, sugar, and doll. He sang old songs from the 40s and 50s. He danced with the women, and women almost fought to hold onto his arm when I bought him in each day. After four weeks, I started receiving calls from the center telling me about my father's behavior. They informed me that they did not have insurance to cover the seniors in case they slipped and fell because of my father's constant singing and dancing. I felt like the mother with the bad child who was constantly being called by the principal's office. They informed me that my father was not welcomed at the center unless I stayed with him every day. Well, I tried it for a week. My father was kicked out of the center.

My father was also kicked out of the senior center in Virginia when he stayed with my sister. He was put out of the center in Charleston, South Carolina, when he stayed with my brother, and he was kicked out of the Marietta, Georgia, center while staying with another sister. So, after four strikes, the word was out; he was not allowed in any center. He was blackballed.

I Don't Know Him, And I Don't Know You Either

My mother was diagnosed with dementia in 2007. My sister bought her to our home, and I prepared dinner and made sure she did not want for nothing. During the visit, I addressed her as mama at least 30 times; however, upon leaving, she told me I was such a nice lady. When I asked her about my dad who was in the bedroom, she had a Color Purple moment, and her reply was "I don't know him, and I don't know you either."

Lord, Please Keep Me In My Right Mind

All my life, I grew up hearing the deacons at church praying. In addition, the prayer always contained the wording "Lord, please keep me in my right mind." I didn't understand what this meant as a young child, but I know now. Over the years, my siblings and I have seen our mom and dad go through the three stages of dementia.

When your mom and dad can't remember their name, cannot remember their own children, and cannot remember how to dress, bath, and groom themselves; cannot even feed themselves, then you completely understand the important of being in your right mind.

Lord, We Thank You For All The Many Blessings

The Lord blessed us with parents who loved us and did the best they could for their children. Perhaps our father was not the best husband, but he was a good father. With the Lord's direction, my father took us out of the projects of Charleston, South Carolina, to Jersey City, New Jersey. This enabled all of us to enjoy a better life than we would have if we stayed in South Carolina.

Most of my sibling now live in the South.

Two live in Wando, South Carolina.

Two live in Clermont, Florida.

One lives in West Palm Beach, Florida.

One lives in Suffolk, Virginia.

One lives in Marietta, Georgia.

One lives in Lunenburg, Massachusetts.

Our parents are both gone now. At the age of 84, my mom went home to be with the Lord on July 21, 2010.

At the age of 90, my daddy passed away on October 24, 2014. We were truly blessed to have our parents in our lives for so many years. I believed we did right by our parents. When they needed us, we were there. As children unable to care for ourselves, our parents fed us, bathed us, clothed us, wiped our mouths, cleaned our noses, and changed our diapers.

How could we not do for them what they did for us? I praise God for every experience He has seen my siblings, and me, safely through. What an amazing God we serve!

Testimony of
William And Katrinka Carlton
Florida
Restoration

I will repay you for the years
the locusts have eaten—the great locust and the
young locust, the other locusts and the
locust swarm—my great army that
I sent among you.

Joel 2:25

Katrinka:

On a cold wintry and snowy morning on January 1, 1990, on my son Dierre Robinson's 20th birthday, at approximately 12:30 a.m., I got a knock on the door from the Akron Ohio Police Department with the news no one wants to hear. The blue uniform spoke for itself. The officer preceded to tell me that my oldest son, Dierre, had been shot and killed by an unidentified shooter. At that time, my heart stopped beating, anxiety rose, fear crept in, and I began to drown in my own tears. My heartrate rushed and began beating out of control. It was like a dream, only reality proved the bad news was true.

As this news began to spread, family and friends rushed to my side, not knowing exactly what had happened or who was the person behind it. All these questions were swimming in my head; our heads. There was weeping and sadness throughout the family when there should have been a birthday celebration. Instead, I faced tears of sadness, unanswered questions, fear, anxiety, and stress, on top of making funeral arrangements and all that comes with a sudden death. Dierre's death was the first death of a brand-new year, 1990.

The news was on the front page of the local newspaper. The neighborhood was shocked, family was shocked, friends were shocked. What seemed to be hours of weeping and crying turned into hours, months, and years of mourning and sadness. Every following New Year brought back those pre-recorded knocks on the door and a reliving of that moment in time, over and over. Every January 1st in the years before Dierre's death had been celebrated with cake and ice cream and happiness. Now, the tables had turned.

As the news traveled from home to home, more concerned and saddened family and friends filled my home with support and encouragement. There were so many unanswered questions. What were his last minutes like? His life was so brief; his death so sudden, so unexpected. Dierre just made it into a new year, and suddenly the lights of life were shut off. I wasn't the same; my kids were not the same. Our lives changed within minutes of a brand-new year.

The unidentified killer was later identified; it seems that Dierre's death was a senseless one of mistaken identity. We were told the killer was out looking for trouble, and he was looking for a young person who matched the similarities of someone who had been in a New Year's fight with his cousin. As Dierre was walking home from his restaurant job, according to a witness, words were exchanged between the two. The killer, sitting in his car, pulled out a gun from the glove compartment and fired the shots. The fatal bullet caught Dierre in the chest. As Dierre began to run for his life, he collapsed and fell dead not far from our home. His death was quick, it was fast, and there was nothing that could have been done to save his life.

New Year's Day began to take on another meaning my family. Every new year was a moment I dreaded, because it was a constant reminder to me. As I rewound those inner tapes, I heard the knock on the door, and the fear, anxiety, and the sadness would grip me again and again, year after year. When celebration should have been taking place, I was mourning behind the doors of my home. My kids and family members helped to carry me through each New Year as we visited his grave (Dierre D. Robinson – Sunrise 1-1-70; Sunset 1-1-90).

Now my family was visiting his grave. And there was more weeping. After six years of sadness on each brand-new New Years' rising, it came to me that I could do something about this continuing sadness and help bring in the new year in a more positive way. I remember this like it was yesterday! I began to think about what I could do to end the continuing sadness and help bring in the new year in a more positive way. I thought about starting a new tradition, bringing in the new year by hosting a women's brunch to help me keep him alive in my heart. Aha!

For 1996, I called a few ladies and invited them to my home , six years after Dierre's death, to start the new year on a positive note. My house was filled with ladies, who helped me redirect my sad thoughts into thoughts of my pleasant memories of my son. We were able to enjoy and recall just how much laughter, fun, and happiness he had lived in his brief moments on earth.

Dierre was loving, he was a joy to be around, he enjoyed a free spirit life, and he was very gifted with his hands. He was such a special child, who loved his dog and enjoyed his younger brother and sister, and he spent lots of time with his family members.

That year, in the midst of my first New Year's brunch, we experienced a visit from the Holy Spirit. That year changed the atmosphere from mourning to joy. There was a new tradition, the old had passed away, behold! God began to do a new thing! Each new year took on a new form; today, it is a celebration of Dierre by an annual gathering entitled The First Fruits. Every new year, on the first Saturday of the new year, is allotted to worship and praise to our Lord and Savior for bringing us through the previous year.

For the past 20 years, remembering Dierre every year on January 1st has turned into a new form of remembering – how God changed everything bad into something as wonderful as the first Fruit celebration. God is worthy, and as we celebrate together His goodness with high praise and worship, we also remember that ashes can be turned into something so beautiful because God is in it all. We rejoice in Dierre's death because Jesus paid it all, and all to Him we owe with praise, testimonies, singing, and worship. What the enemy meant for evil, God was turning around for His good.

In prayer, God gave the name, *First Fruits* to be retained as an annual event. Year after year, people began to look forward to starting out the new year at this First Fruit event, praising and worshiping God for the good things He is doing. Dierre's death turned the dark days into light days. Each brand-new year is a time of praise, worship, fellowshipping, and enjoying the First Fruit with the fruit of the spirit operating in the midst of God's people, rejoicing and singing!

You see, we never know why a tragedy happens, but God can turn ashes into beauty if a person is willing. I realized that something as bad as death could be used for a good thing, and Dierre's death has turned out to bless so many lives because Jesus is the center of the celebration. First Fruit has been in existence since 1996, and continues every year, worshipping, praising, and testifying to the goodness of Jesus Christ, our Lord and Savior.

How I Met William

As my life continued to unfold, the stakes changed tremendously in the 1998. To my pleasant surprise, I was introduced at my church to a handsome man by the name of William Carlton. William and I met in the Sunday School class at a church in Ohio, noted by the name of The House of the Lord. After William observed my lifestyle and love for God, and discovered I was single, he approached me to see if I would be interested in going out on a date. And after a series of phone conversations, we figured out that we enjoyed each other's conversation, and we made a date to have dinner together.

The evening turned out to be so wonderful, as he pulled up in the driveway in a black long-stretched limousine for our first big date. Now that was certainly a huge surprise to me. It was a new beginning in our lives, all designed and created by Our Father in Heaven. It was such a night of fun, great food, entertainment, and laughter, after enjoying a fun-filled night of limo riding down in the Flats in Cleveland, Ohio, where we dined at a very exclusive restaurant on Lake Erie at Pier W. What a night to remember! And what a new turn in my life, as we continued dating for two years and became one of the first couples to engage in holy matrimony for the year 2000. The entire church of over 300 guests arrived to help celebrate this joyous occasion together in the presence of the Lord. We have been happily married now for over 19 years of love and great joy. We minister to the hurting, lost, abused, and confused all to the glory of the Lord.

We moved to the Florida area in the 2013 and have continued to enjoy life together along with a huge number of friends we've met since relocating from Ohio to the Lakeland area. My life truly is reflective of redemption and restoration. William and I have a blended family of seven grown children, eight grandchildren, and seven great-grandchildren.

William:

> One thing have I desired of the Lord,
> that will I seek after; that I may dwell in the
> house of the Lord all the days of my life,
> to behold the beauty of the Lord,
> and to enquire in his temple.

Psalms 27:4

Lord, your grace and mercy have followed me all the days of my life, and I continuously praise your holy name! Ever since I was a child, you have blessed me. You blessed me with a godly mother, who instilled in me a consciousness that you were real; though when I was younger, I did not understand. When she took us to church, my siblings and I heard about you, but we really did not know you. I could not wait until I got a little older, unknown to my mother; I was able to sneak out of church. Religion did not mean that much to me. When I was a teenager in high school, I saw a beautiful girl whom I fell in love with at first sight. I knew she was the one for me. Every time I saw her something inside of me made me feel like singing a song:

> God has smiled on me; who caused my heart to jump for joy. Her beauty would cause the purple lilies in the field to bow in adoration. The sound of her voice was so soft and melodious. Her smile would radiate like a a bright light in any room. How I wish that God would bless me one day and she would only be mine.

I later found out that special girl felt the same way about me. We dated for several months. Like many teenagers in love, our intense passion moved us to another level of intimacy. Shortly thereafter, both of our lives turned upside down when we discovered she was pregnant. I knew I was not ready to handle the responsibility of parenthood. However, when the baby girl was born, I felt so happy and proud. She was so beautiful and meant the world to me. The pressure of fatherhood still was a heavy burden, and our love relationship turned into harsh arguments. I wanted to be free, so I joined the U.S. Army.

While in the service, during my lonely moments, I reflected upon how difficult it was for me and my siblings growing up without the presence and support of my father. I did not want my daughter to grow up with that type of experience. Upon being honorably discharged from the military, I wanted to do the honorable thing with the mother of my child. We reconciled and later got married. Those days were sometimes good, and at other times rather rocky. However, we stayed together. We were blessed to bring several children into the world. Even though I tried to settle down, I still wanted to live a free spirit life. I drove my motorcycle, drank a little, and spent time away from home.

Going to church was not a priority for my family, nor for me. Until one day, as I was driving my motorcycle, I had to pull over. I was overwhelmed with the thought that it was time for me to get right with God and set a spiritual foundation for my family. When I was a child, I heard it said by several old deacons testifying in church "the prayers of my mother followed me ..." I think this is what happened to me. I started my motorcycle and drove back home. Upon reaching home, I gathered my children and wife and informed them that we are going back to church. Strangely enough, I believe that going back to church and trying to live right before God was the starting point of new, unexpected good times; as well as the intensified, painful challenges in my family's life.

We were blessed to have our own home and be surrounded by family and friends. Sometimes our home, as with many new families, was not peaceful due to the tensions between my wife and me. I spent 16 hours a day at my job. My wife earned her college degree and worked full time. This left us with little time for each other. Gradually our love and trust for each other began to drift. Moreover, I experienced a major change in my life, which gave me an unwanted and unexpected understanding of my wedding vow.

"I promise to love her, comfort her, honor and keep her for better or worse, for richer or poorer, in sickness and health ... until death do us part."

A family's life can be turned upside down when the unwelcome visitors of sickness and death come to visit. That is what happened to my family. It left my wife with a major life-threatening condition, required two serious heart operations. Sometimes I felt so helpless, I did not know what to do, but I remembered my mother teaching me, "prayer changes things." Because I felt closer to the Lord, I, along with my children prayed and prayed and prayed, and even anointed my wife with holy oil. We were convinced that the Lord heard our prayers, and I truly believed that my wife would recover. However, one evening my wife was rushed to the hospital. Later that evening the surgeon told me that despite their best efforts, she nonetheless had passed. I felt as though someone had just stabbed me in the heart and was pulling the knife out. My world collapsed.

My pain became even more excruciating when I gathered my children. How was I to tell them that our prayers were in vain? For some reason, God chose not to hear them. The days after that event, and the many years after her funeral, left a deep void in my soul. I felt so betrayed and all alone. My wife and I were married for 30 years. Even though I could not understand why I was left to raise our three remaining sons alone, and to go through this type of pain, nonetheless I believed God was still with me and would see me through …

In my quest to find inner peace, I joined a church where I felt comfortable and was spiritually fed. I met new people who had genuine respect and love for each other. While there, I met a beautiful, effervescent woman whose love for the Lord was apparent to everyone. I could not take my eyes away from her. I felt as though I was being captured by her radiant beauty and gracious spirit. Without a doubt, the Lord heard my prayer, and sent someone to make me laugh again, someone to help me find joy again, someone who would love my family, and me, for who we are. The Lord did just that! He allowed me to form a genuine love relationship with Katrinka Robinson.

We discovered that we had so many things in common; she also had life-changing experiences. However, the Lord carried her through each one of them. We soon fell in love and sought to get married. There were several major obstacles to our desire, but we believed that the Lord would work them all out.

I came to fully believe what the saints of old would always say, "The Lord moves in mysterious ways ... there is nothing impossible for God to do." A few months later, I traveled to Israel. While there, I visited the Wailing Wall. I inserted my prayer request, asking for Katrinka and me to get married. We wanted God's will to be done. Upon my arrival home, and after a brief meeting with the pastor, we discovered that all of the obstacles to marriage were resolved. Hallelujah!

On April 1, 2000, we married. Ever since that day, God has smiled upon our lives. We have traveled different parts of the world. We shop together; she has even changed my wardrobe into bright shirts, shorts, sneakers, hats, sunglasses, etc. She brings sunshine, joy, and peace into my life. Most importantly, she ignites my love for the Lord, and I have a burning desire to do God's will. I am so glad and proud to say that all my children and grandchildren have come to know the Lord for themselves. I have eight children, six grandchildren, and seven great-grandchildren. This is why I can honestly testify God's grace and mercy has followed me all the days of my life, and as long as I live, I will praise God's holy name. Hallelujah!

Testimony of
Debbie Barney
Georgia
There's Only One Way

But you will receive power when the
Holy Spirit has come upon you, and you will be
my witness in Jerusalem and in all Judea and
Samaria, and to the end of the earth...

Acts 1:8

Time quickly passes by all of us; it pauses for no
one. Sometimes it only leaves us with precious
and priceless memories. This morning, I asked myself
a rather unusual question. "How did I get here, and
where exactly is here?" As I began to reflect and write,
tears formed in my eyes and began to stream down my
cheeks. The answer became as clear as day. I am here and
writing because the inconceivable happened. Without
warning, and in the blink of an eye, she was gone. My
baby was gone, and life as I knew it, had forever been
changed.

My mind wanders back to January 17, 2015. It was
the second worst day of my life. This was the day we laid

my child to rest. I still couldn't wrap my head around what was happening. Here I was, sitting on a metal chair in the front row of the church, staring at my baby lying in a casket. I asked myself time and time again; how was I able to sit there composed and contain the agony I felt inside? What prevented me from running up to her and wrapping my arms around her lifeless body? What prevented my hands from clutching at her arms and holding onto her tightly for the very last time, refusing to let go until my hands were physically pried from her? Surely, I expected my heart to stop beating at any moment, and I could be released from the reality of her sudden death and knowing I would live my life without her. I asked myself, how was that possible?

At the ceremony, I sat still on my chair, staring at her and taking in everything while I still could. I wanted to memorize every detail about how she looked, how her hair was styled, her flawless makeup, just the right amount of jewelry, the clothes she was wearing, and even the color of her lipstick and fingernails. Yes, everything about her was perfect. She was a portrait of sheer beauty, and her face glowed with a peace I had never seen before. I heard people comment how she looked like an angel. She was my real-life sleeping beauty, and I desperately prayed that she would wake up. I sat and silently pleaded within myself, please Che', please wake up!

I listened intently to the message my pastor spoke, not ever wanting him to finish; because I knew once he was done they were going to get into position to take her away.

I recall him reading scripture from the book of John, and I clung to every word he said as though they were the instructions as to how I was going to proceed with my life from here. The eulogy was so powerful. I felt an immediate connection to what God had clearly given my pastor not only to edify my spirit, but also to include a word for every individual seated in the sanctuary that cold, winter day. Although I felt the bitter sting of grief and sorrow building up within me, it did not overcome me. That was all God; he blocked it. To be honest, I felt an urge to stand, raise my hands, and give God praise. Again, how was this possible? I didn't understand it, but I embraced it. I didn't expect it, but I was blessed by it. I can't even begin to explain how any of it happened, but it did. It happened.

Clearly God took over my body and my actions, preventing me from losing control and breaking down.

Instead, He allowed his Holy Spirit to intervene on my behalf, casting aside the hardship and devastation of what could have been the darkest hours of my entire life. What should have been an unbearable and helpless time for me somehow wasn't. God's mercy and His amazing grace reigned down on me and my family that homegoing day, and it shone bright throughout the sanctuary for all to see.

I remember Pastor saying during the eulogy if you want to be close to your loved one, you must be close to God. Those words resonated repeatedly in my mind for many days to come. Was what he said true? If I got close to God, somehow, I would be closer to my child? I wanted this to be true. I needed this to be true! I needed to be as close to her as possible if I was going to get through this. I decided right then that I was going to expedite the process. I wasn't going to take my time. I wasn't going to walk. I was going to run towards God, and run is exactly what I did!

The week dragged by and showed no mercy. The days were hard, and yet the nights considerably harder. I was caught up in the pain and couldn't wrap my head around it all. It was too much for me to bear, and I was compelled to consider what options I had in front of me.

I could succumb to the trauma, giving in and losing everything that meant anything to me. This included my family, my belief in God, my will to live, my destiny, and my purpose in life, which would result in defeat.

How could I be a witness, a living testimony, a faithful disciple spreading the good news of God and the glory of His coming kingdom if I was unable to stand this test in time? A test that challenges every fiber of my being; mind, body, and soul! A test that I am able and often willing to fail due to the enormity of it. The loss I bore became more than me; more than my life, my sanity, who I thought I was, or what I found to be surreal and inconceivable!

I have come to realize that because of who God is, He knows and understands the depth and extent of my suffering. The separation from my child is painful; my heart aches, and I miss her as deeply and as fiercely as one can be missed. Somehow, God made what I once felt to be unbearable, bearable; what seemed impossible, possible; what was once meaningless, meaningful. I don't know how, other than by the power of His might, He is able to transform my grief into his glory! My spirit tells me that they who wait on the Lord shall renew their strength; they shall mount up with wings like eagles;

they shall run and not be weary; they shall walk and not faint. I believe what His word says, and that it is He, who sustains me through it all, my desperation for my child has ultimately become my desperation for God!

Testimony of
Cindi Gomes
New York
**A Walk In The Dark,
Shed Light On My Life**

The Lord is near to those who have a broken heart,
and saves such as have a contrite spirit.
Many are the afflictions of the righteous;
But the Lord delivers him out of them all.

Psalm 34:18-19

One of the gifts of youth is a carefree sense of freedom and hope for the future. It can be a worry-free time of life unaffected by personal tragedy, except for the things that happen in the news or to "other" people. I had a good, fun-filled youth while occasionally a member of my large extended family passed on. Generally, I was not deeply impacted by death; it came to older members of the family and followed a natural progression of the circle of life.

My perspective on death and dying was radically altered by a phone call late one night. I was a teenager and the phone rang and woke me from my sleep. I heard my mother answer and gasp in horror; she quickly got dressed and left the house. My cousin, a high schooler, was killed in a tragic car crash. This struck very close to home because I loved him and he was young like me, and now for the first time, I became afraid of death. I realized that death did not discriminate and could happen to anyone at any time.

I always went to church and believed in God. I accepted Jesus Christ as my lord and savior in high school. I applied my faith to my life throughout high school, college, and adulthood. For many years, while I did not conscientiously practice a Christian "lifestyle," I believed I had deeply rooted values in my faith. When life brought me ups, I felt grateful and when life brought me downs, I stayed faithful. I never lost faith in God, no matter what trials came my way. However, once out of college and into adulthood, the ease of youthful expectations and hope for a future of easy living was no longer taken for granted or certain. Life-altering realities brought many fearful and painful changes to my life. Now I contend daily with real, devastating effects of many tragic losses and unfulfilled dreams.

On August 28, 2001, I found my younger sister in the basement of my home unresponsive. She was pronounced dead right there. Moreover, two weeks later and literally to the day and time of my sister Kim's passing, on September 11, 2001, two planes flew into the World Trade Center. This was 911 and thousands of people perished or were critically wounded. I was utterly traumatized by these events.

I lived just minutes across the Hudson River on the New Jersey side, where the river divides New York City and New Jersey. I could see the Manhattan skyline and the World Trade Center on my daily commute along Boulevard East, which runs parallel to the Hudson river. I am a Sound Engineer for CBS News and I had just returned to work the day before from bereavement time off. Suddenly, I was thrust into providing coverage of this huge national tragedy which piled onto my own personal grief and loss. Ironically my original work assignment was to be down by the World Trade Center the morning of 9/11, but by the grace of God, my assignment was changed the night before to a different location. We had just reached the Red Cross Blood bank in Philadelphia when we heard the news. As we raced back toward NYC on the New Jersey Turnpike, we watched in horror the World Trade Center towers come down. For the next several weeks, my news team covered numerous memorial services for people who perished in the tragedy. We attended services one after the other for people we did not know. It was emotionally draining and I had no time to process my own personal grief for my sister, Kim. The stress of suppressing my feelings for so long was taking it's toll but I pressed on to work day after day without complaint.

My faith was shaken to its core. I thought to myself, what is going on? How in the world will I be able to handle all these things and still have peace of mind? The truth of the matter is I could not. I could not reconcile my feelings, having so many layers of loss, guilt, fear, and anger. My days were filled with sadness, spiraling me downward into moments of confusion and despair. I was not able to rely on my faith because it had never been tested in this way, and I was emotionally, physically, and spiritually weak. I was unprepared to deal with the enormity of these events. My path was bleak for several months, even years. It seemed to be a lifetime before I was able to process and accept my sister Kim's death. The uncertainty and value of life on this planet became a long and often lonely, unresolved struggle. It took years of sharing my struggles with my best friends before I gradually found my way back to having peace of mind and balance. I accepted the fact that life was not going to be easy or perfect and longevity of life is not a given nor promised to anyone.

I don't think anyone recovers 100 percent from a loss or tragedy and the cliché "time heals all wounds" is true to an extent. I believe that the loss of a loved one leaves a deep void in one's soul; we regain some degree of peace and simply learn how to cope. I believe our existence on earth is a journey to faith. If we follow God's guiding principles we can get through a crisis and sustain a healthy and meaningful life. Storms, trials, tests, and afflictions may still come.

Many years passed and once again, I was able to smile, laugh, and enjoy most aspects of my life. I tried to live my life being appreciative, grateful, and reasonably happy with family, friends, and situations. Like everybody, I have had my share of up's and downs, but through them all, God has always been my source of strength. However, life is a continuous circle where experiences of the past seem to recycle, both good and bad. My hope and resilience would be tested again but his time it would bring relentless and much deeper painful intrusions, not only within me, but into the lives of my family and closest friends. I could not have imagined, let alone believe, the things that happened. My faith was stretched again almost to the breaking point. Even though I was now older, much wiser, and a little stronger in my walk of faith, nothing could prepare me for what was to come. The trials and ordeals were so intimidating, I even wondered if my degree of faith was able to sustain me through the onslaught of endless, back-to-back loss. At times, I felt as though mercy abandoned me, and there was no hope or light of day in sight.

October 2014. I was driving back to New York from Washington D.C. and I had an amazing weekend. I had reconnected with an old friend; well, frankly, an old flame and I was on cloud nine. I had not felt connected with anyone for a very long time, but we had history; it had been years since we saw or spoke to each other and I was excited about the possibility of finding love again. I was ecstatic and this was a full circle moment. However, this ecstasy would be short lived. Life was about to come full circle all right, but not in the manner I imagined.

Within a few miles of reaching home, my phone rang, and it was my best friend's husband. The next phase of testing came abruptly, and my feeling of excitement quickly turned to horror in a matter of seconds. He was in a panic and told me that he and his daughter were rushing my sweet best friend, Wendy, to the hospital, and I needed to meet them there as soon as possible. I knew she had been sick with mononucleosis and some other lingering issues for months, but this development sounded more serious. I raced to the hospital, and Wendy was in full kidney and liver decline. Within 24 hours, she was diagnosed with leukemia and lymphoma, and was immediately transferred to another hospital (Hackensack Medical Center). She needed aggressive medical attention and the prognosis wasn't good. After a few days, there where signs of improvement, so the doctors could begin the next phase of treating the cancer. I went to the hospital every single day for several weeks, all the way to Thanksgiving. We prepared a great dinner to take to the hospital to celebrate Thanksgiving with her; however, on the eve before Thanksgiving, Wendy came down with a high fever, resulting from what the doctor called a "super bug." Her immune system was too weak, and she succumbed on Friday, November 28, 2014, the night after Thanksgiving. In tears and disbelief, we gathered by her side and said goodbye. It was devastating. I left the hospital at 3am and on the drive home a deep fog encircled me; the trauma of those last moments with one of my most beloved friends set in.

Wendy was like a sister to me, and all the feelings of my sister Kim's passing came right back to haunt me. With no time to absorb or grieve, I became consumed with the planning of her memorial service.

The few weeks after the funeral were a blur, but once I returned to work, I received a lot of support from my colleagues and I got on with it. My faith and sense of balance was restored and I accepted that God's will was done; no matter how painful and untimely it seemed to me. By faith, I accepted it.

On January 15, 2015, just barely six weeks later, the pendulum would swing again and I received another dreadful phone call late in the night.

Let me first preface my challenges with this brief comment. I am blessed with longstanding friendships; most since elementary school. They are my cherished friendships even today. Although we live many miles apart, we love each other unconditionally. This part of my testimony reflects the level of faith in God and each other found at our small church in Brockton, Massachusetts. That experience was the bond of love. That love held us together as best friends as we each walked through our own difficult and painful paths of life.

Once again, my phone rang, and this time it is my best friend Leeanna with dreadful news about another one of our best friends, Debbie. Her youngest daughter, LeChe, had a brain aneurysm and did not survive.

Could this really be happening all over again? We just gathered for Wendy's home going only a few weeks ago. I was completely shocked, dismayed, and stunned that it was happening again. I wondered where is God?! Wendy, a young mother, just died and left behind a young daughter at a most vulnerable age; now, Debbie, a young mother, lost her young daughter, leaving her a devastated mother. What kind of twisted fate is this?

The questions continuously swirled around in my mind, and I was at loss for words to explain this new twist of life to anybody, let alone my colleagues or my boss. Another tragedy? It was surreal! Once again, I rallied support for my beautiful sister friend Debbie and her family. It was overwhelming and hard to fathom as being real, but it was. I again felt unsure about my faith; but although I was shaken, I was not shattered. I pressed on, hoping to reconcile my doubt because I believed that God would not forsake us. At some point, God would make clear to each of us the reason for these tragic events. I came to realize that it would take some time for me to grasp what life affirming lessons I was supposed to learn, aside from the heartache.

Meanwhile, another storm was brewing back home in Massachusetts. It was like an endless hurricane season, where the storms keep coming one after the other, each following the exact same path of destruction. Upon my arrival home, coming back from Erie, Pennsylvania, I was confronted with the saddest news of my life. While in the longest, sustained period of personal tragedy I could imagine, my mom called to tell me that my youngest brother, Mark, at 49-years-old, was diagnosed with pancreatic cancer; one of the most aggressive and painful forms of cancer. The survival rate is 4 percent. We knew he had expressed different levels of physical discomfort, but we never thought it was life threatening. To be honest, I literally thought, "what the hell;" I cannot take any more bad news.

Without a doubt or a moment of hesitation, even though I was exhausted, I knew I had to be there in Massachusetts for my baby brother. At this point, I cannot process my emotions anymore, and frankly, I am numb. I felt like I was cast down into hell, falling down a pit of sadness and grief, and I did not care if I could get out. I laid constricted and emotionally paralyzed in the abyss of tragedy and fear. My heart could not hurt any more than it already did; I knew I needed God more than ever before, but how was I to find him?

I felt embarrassment that once again, I had to explain these happenings to people. I had to go to my boss again and ask for time to go to Boston to help with my family. Amazingly, my boss understood my unusual circumstances and out of compassion, afforded me the opportunity to work in Boston for as long as I needed. While in Boston, I accompanied Mark to his first appointment with his oncologist. The diagnosis was grim; even with the most aggressive treatment, he may only have a year to live. It took everything in my power not to completely fall to pieces, right there and then, but I knew I had to be strong for my brother and my mom, so I held myself together.

Why, why, why, was all I could think? First Wendy, then LeChe, and now my baby brother will more than likely only see his 50th birthday, and that was unfathomable. If I ever felt like God had forsaken us, now might be the time. However, something happened. My friends' and family who were either indirectly or directly affected by each tragedy formed this circle of comfort, strength, and hope for one another. We were all dealing with loss, so we needed each other. Therefore, we were sensitive to one another in way that was different from an isolated event. When that happens; you give support but move on. Now, the succession of events were keeping us close and binding us together in an amazing way; we were rediscovering our faith in God in a more powerful way, together.

Yes, adversity is real, and it is painful, but we were all going through it at the same time. Although the burden was great and overwhelming, I started to see light on the other side. I realized that God is not forsaking us, and I felt that these tragic events were bringing us closer together and closer to Him. I felt closer to God while going through my brother's illness and knowing God in a way I never did. It was not simply out of need; it was out of love. My prayers were different. I saw miracles in my brother's journey that I could not have seen had I not rediscovered my faith in God. I was feeling God's presence in ways I never had; and simply put, things happened during the last few weeks of Mark's life that can only be explained as God's mercy. I watched my brother's decline, and it was excruciatingly painful. I do not wish that for anyone. I will always have a void in my heart for every loss I endured, but I strive and hunger for peace and understanding under the most difficult circumstances; otherwise, I can't live out the rest of my life in a meaningful way. I do not want to oversimplify or imply that God sacrificed others to bring us closer to him, but I believe there are teachable moments during the most difficult times if we are open to see them. We must trust and have faith in God's plan.

One day, while sitting on Mark's bed, we were talking about his legacy. He was sad, expressing his feelings of not having any children, and I was comforting him. I was impressed by the number of friends Mark had, and the overwhelming support they gave him. It was truly impressive and remarkable how much he was loved. I told him he had a legacy; it was playing out before him, and that he was lucky to be able to see that. In the same conversation, I said, Mark, you are not alone. We all bare the cross in some form; none of us will be spared. Yes, he was suffering this illness, but it could happen to any one of us next. It was a foreshadow moment, for little did I know, in fact, it would be me!

Mark passed on January 18, 2016; and less than a year later, I was diagnosed with breast cancer on January 3, 2017.

It was another full circle moment. I literally stood and looked out the window from the very same hospital where this whole journey began at Hackensack Medical Center; the same hospital where Wendy passed in 2014. I had every emotion and fear one would have given this diagnosis. This time, the questions swirled around my mind, but it was my fate. Is this it, am I going to die from this affliction? A myriad of scary thoughts flowed in and out of my mind. Immediately, I was thrust into a state of shock and before I could do anything about it, my brain shifted into emotional shut down mode. It was very hard for me to believe what I had just been told. Coincidently, my boss called and caught me at this vulnerable moment. Here I was again, sharing more bad news. I actually felt embarrassed telling him I had breast cancer, but I could not keep the trauma of those moments to myself. To this day, he does not know the magnitude of my gratitude for his compassion, and that he was the first person I told.

While standing in that room, gazing out the window, I remembered the conversation I had with Mark that day; now, here I was. It was as if I had a premonition that I would be challenged with a life-altering affliction. Now, the possibility of death stared me in the face, too.

After a few minutes, I wiped my tears, composed myself, and headed home. The drive was like the night I left the hospital after Wendy died. It felt like a fog engulfing me again on the longest drive of my life.

I spent two years trying to take care of other people, which I would not change for anything in the world, but I also neglected my own health for years. I was sick for a long time, physically, emotionally, and spiritually. I felt beaten, tired, and weary, and this affliction could defeat me, or I could rise to the challenge and fight it. I did not know how I would muster the will and determination to do it, but I decided that this could shape the rest of my life for good. While going through endless and painful needle biopsies, where I had to lay flat on my belly in the most uncomfortable positions, I had a visualization. I saw myself as a child and imagined that I was walking hand-in-hand with Jesus. I could literally see a little girl walking with Jesus. It was my younger self. I never felt so safe, and this restored my faith and cast away any doubt I had. I had an unwavering faith that I would get through this with God's mercy. I simply lived one day at a time. I had a double mastectomy and chemotherapy for several months. At one point, I got so sick and frail that I ended up back in Hackensack Medical Center, on the exact same oncology floor where I spent several weeks with Wendy. This caused discomfort because it was surreal; but the hospital provided me with amazing nurses, doctors, and spiritual support. Most importantly, I kept my faith!

No Other Way

For me, my journey took me back to the beginning. I had to walk with Jesus and recommit my life to him. The culmination of two years of unimaginable tragedy brought grief and despair but I found hope and resilience. Even as I write today, there are still challenges with my health and in my life, but I learned how to live in the moment, one day at a time. What used to be a cliché is now how I try to live my life each day. I have a sense of freedom that I never appreciated before, because I have accepted the things I cannot control or change; and while I admit, I am not FEARLESS, at least I know today, I am not FEARFUL. God has blessed me in so many ways, and I am grateful. Donnie McClurkin's song We Fall Down, But We Get Up is my mantra. I only hope and pray for continued grace, and that I stay grounded and rooted in my faith...I do not know any other way.

Testimony of
Dr. Col. Tracy Ringo
Ohio
**Trials Don't Break You,
They Just Make You Better**

Trust in the Lord with all of your heart
and lean not on your own understanding;
in all your ways submit to him
and he will make your paths straight.

Proverbs 3: 5-6

I put this verse to practice without being very aware of the scripture until recent years. What I mean by that is, you can read the Bible, and depending on where you are in your faith or walk with God, you may get a different interpretation of the same scripture; or it just sticks with you, because you finally get it! The words become more than just letters on a page; they become a part of your being. Trust in the Lord, not in man nor woman. We have to walk by faith and not by sight. When we put this scripture to action and allow God's will in our life, we can rest assured that we will live a fully purposeful life, with the fewest number of detours and roadblocks. When we go through trying times, we all tend to call a friend or family member to get their opinions. They offer us the best advice they can give at the time, maybe! Our opinions of life situations are based on our experiences, and so you may be asking for advice from someone who can actually make your situation more confusing, or it may have a negative outcome due to just bad advice. I refer to asking multiple people for advice about your situation as background noise. The noise gets so loud, with all of it's confusing and complicated sounds, it can make situations or issues even more stressful. It is a natural instinct to want to talk with someone about your problems, but why not talk to someone who is all-knowing, who knows the best path to take, who already knows the outcome, and who will always point you in the right direction? Take your burdens to the Lord and lay them down. So simple, yet so hard for most.

When we face issues in our lives, it may seem that if we are not actively worrying, we are not working on solving the issue; yet while worrying, there is usually no problem-solving happening, we are just stressing ourselves with the problem and every negative outcome we can imagine. What does worrying do? Worrying does nothing but weigh on your spirit, and most likely, have you make bad choices or decisions in the process. Worrying can make you ill and cause physical damage to your body. Most often, this is manifest in the stomach or gut. We are unable to eat, or we eat more than we should. Our bowels become overactive or have no activity at all. Think about every situation that you ever worried about; what was the outcome? Did worrying change the outcome, or did it just make you a bundle of unproductive nerves? Being able to give your problem to the Lord is truly a great gift. You have the opportunity to show others that even though I am going through a storm, I am able to be positive, productive, and peaceful! When you have relationship issues, employment issues, and/ or family issues, you may not tell others exactly what is going on, but they have some idea about your struggles or the obstacles you are enduring. It is how we handle the storms that shows our faith. Can we praise God in the midst of the storm? Can we be grateful and thankful for the ability to navigate the storm, knowing that we will be better for it in the end? Storms are struggles, trials, and tribulations. I can look back on every storm in my life and see that I learned an invaluable lesson, came out stronger and wiser, and most of all, I survived!

When we are Christians, we are being watched for how we deal with situations. We give others advice, but do we practice what we preach? I have had major storms in my life. I remember wanting to be physician since I was 12 years old. My maternal grandmother, who was my everything, was diagnosed with cancer. Being so young at the time, my thoughts were God knows, she is the glue in this family and knows we would be lost without her, so surely she will be fine. I watched my grandmother die so quickly after being diagnosed with cancer that I thought the doctors did not do enough for her. It made me not want to see anyone else die from such a horrible disease. I was going to find a cure for cancer! What I later realized is that her fear of doctors and late detection of her disease was the real reason she died so quickly. My focus went from finding a cure for cancer to early detection and prevention of the disease. Every time I speak with a patient about preventative care, I remember how I wish my own grandmother had that same advice. It is my own way of honoring my grandmother and keeping alive the dream of a 12 year old to do something to help others, so no one would suffer like my grandmother. I always had my family's support, and I was always told I could be anything I wanted to be with hard work and dedication. I then set out to expose myself to everything medical related.

I went to the Army and became a medic at the age of

18. The military helped me pay for college and gave me even more experience, confidence, and structure in my life to be successful.

When it was time to go to my undergraduate counselor at the university I attended for advice on medical school application and process, I was told to pick a different career path in medicine because I had two strikes against me! The two strikes that he, as a white caucasian male, was referring to were that I was black and a female! He handed me a blue and white pamphlet, 200 Careers in the Medical Field! I graciously handed him the pamphlet back and proceeded to find myself another guidance counselor. I often wonder how many other intelligent and capable people this man deflated and demoralized with his prejudices and preconceived notion that you are only as capable as the color of your skin. By this time, I had prepared myself for six years to be a physician by taking college preparatory classes in high school, working as a nurse's assistant in the evenings while still in high school, and by attending every medical preparatory summer program available to me. I now had the doubt of not being good enough forced upon me by someone who was supposed to be encouraging and a mentor. I quickly dropped to my knees and asked God to lead me. I could not see myself pursuing any other career than that of a physician. I then decided that I would whole-heartedly pursue my career as a physician and believed that God would show me what direction I should go, and that He had not brought me this far to leave me! I went back to the university I attended and found another guidance counselor, who was also a white male.

This time, he looked at my credentials and all that I had done up until that point, and he said to me, not only do I think you will make a great physician, it would be my honor to write you a letter of recommendation for your entrance application to medical school. Years later, after graduating medical school, during my residency program, I was married and pregnant with my first child. I thought I should wait until graduation to start a family; but my colleagues were starting families and made it look so easy that I thought, why not start a family? I was in my last year of training and was pregnant at the same time with another administrator at the hospital. My pregnancy was very difficult, and I had to use IV medications to stop me from having morning sickness which lasted all day and night for six months until I delivered my daughter Brooke Lynn prematurely.

I had an emergency cesarean section on Christmas Day and she was born at 12:30 a.m. On December 26, 2001. Brooke had a severe pneumonia and died in the hospital shortly after she was born. I still remember the pain, the intensity and sharpness of the pain. The pain was like a knife that cut so deep right to my heart. Every second was a challenge to just breathe. I was not sure how I was going to make it through this storm. God sent so many people to comfort me and encourage me, and I let them do just that! What I knew this time was that this was the greatest pain I had ever endured and that I would have to do things different. Sometimes we tend to push people away to deal with our issues, grieve, and have our pain in private putting on a brave face in public.

Once people found out about my loss, they begin to share about the same thing happening to them. I had known these people for years but never knew they had lost a child. They prayed for me and shared the story of the same situation they had faced years ago. Those sharing their story allowed me to see that it is possible to make it through. Their hope for me was that I would help the next person in my same situation be able to see that there is life after such a tragic loss. I became a better person and a more compassionate physician because of my daughter Brooke Lynn. She was here for only a short period but affected my life in such a major way. I was told to keep a journal of those days after her passing, which is something that I had never done. I read the entries and it is amazing how far God has brought me. I went from not knowing if I could withstand taking another painful breath to being able to cherish the little time we had and encourage others in my situation. I held on strong to God's words and found peace in knowing that even though Brooke could not come back to me, I would be reunited with her again. Withoutmy faith and knowing that, God has a purpose for us, where would I be. Lost is the first word to come to my mind. I remember praying to God to not allow me to be sad when I see other babies and please God do not allow me to be sad at Christmas time. He answered my prayers! We have choices and I chose to be positive. I know just how precious life is. I use to take pregnancy for granted; you get pregnant and deliver a healthy baby, right? No, not for some, life is precious and the birth of a child is truly a blessing from God.

What I was able to learn from this experience years later was that I had to go through this in order to the compassionate and caring physician that I am today. I always thought I was those things but God's grace and favor elevated me to another level.

The ability to trust God in all situations is key. We know that His love supersedes all love and that He only wants the best for us. I tell my son, if you are good to people all the time, good things will happen to you, most of the time. We as Christians are not exempt from tragedy; it is how we navigate the storms that set us apart from others. We are always thanking God for the good times, but to be thankful to God during our low periods is truly when we have arrived in our spiritual journey. I am thankful that I had time with my daughter even if it was just for a moment. She molded me into the women that I am today, she changed the stride in my step. Brooke's pure existence brought me closer to my Lord and Savior because the depth of pain I felt could not have been healed by anyone here on this earth. I had to feel the pain to get to the other side, which was joy and peace! My advice would be not to try and dull the pain, let the pain exist, feel it, live it, breathe it and then ... Let it go! Replacing your pain with peace and understanding will surely break you and make you better, and if you can be better for yourself, you can be better for others around you! I now see life as an adventure.

I do not fear the unknown because if God can get me through losing my daughter, He can get me through anything!

But He said to me: My grace is sufficient for you, for my power is made perfect in weakness. Therefore, I will boast all the more gladly about my weaknesses, so that Christ's power may rest on me. (2 Corinthians 12: 9)

Surround yourself with all things positive. Feed your soul with the word of God and listen to music that is glorifying and uplifting. Begin and end your day with prayer, be grateful for the small things in life. Love yourself, take care of yourself, mentally, physically and spiritually. My prayer is that people will see God in me. That I will walk in a manner that appears unfamiliar yet interesting to drawn others in. I give praise to God and give Him all the glory for the person I am today. Without God, there would be no me.

My Hope es in the Lord God!
en the Lord God!
Jesus is Our Savior!.
Love!
Dr. Coralotta Darwin   12/13/19

Testimony of
Rev. Dr. Coralotta Darwin
Massachusetts
Transformed

For though we walk in the flesh,
we do not war after the flesh:
For the weapons of our warfare are not carnal,
but mighty through God to the pulling down of
strongholds; casting down imaginations,
and every high thing that exalted itself against
the knowledge of God, and bringing into captivity
every thought to the obedience of Christ;
and having in a readiness to revenge all disobedience,
when your obedience is fulfilled.

2 Corinthians 10:3-6

What's a girl like me doing in a place like this?

If I can describe the spiritual, mental, and physical affliction and abuse one encounters when addiction is at its worst, here is an image I view as a partial list of the overwhelming vicious cycle of pain.

Recalling the very last time I used is extremely difficult. I experienced memory loss. One day, while I was living in Bridgewater, Massachusetts, I was involved with a man in an abusive toxic relationship. After he went to work (on the overnight shift), and after putting my son to bed for the night, I took a trip to Brockton to buy crack cocaine. I knew the clock was ticking on using drugs before he arrived home in the morning from work. As I made it back to the house, I decided to take a detour and go sit on a park bench above the apartment complex. I reached in my pocket for my glass stem (drug paraphernalia) and inserted some of the rock cocaine to smoke! Immediately, I experienced euphoria, numbness, psychosis ... which did not last but a few minutes. From there, I arrived home to finish smoking the rest of the rock cocaine. It wasn't long before paranoia crept in.

I was afraid I was going to be discovered by my man. I had to escape. What I did was pack up my bags, in panic mode, and reached out to my mother that I needed to come home from the abusive man in my life. My addiction had become so insidious, I was a mad woman, sick, broken, depressed, downtrodden, mental slavery, troubling, strange, weird, confused, fallen, beyond belief, desperate, manipulating, lying, aggravated, bondage, absurd, hopeless, neurotic, emotional, destructive, witchcraft, diabolical, demonic, denial, shattered, hopeless, paralyzing fear, guilt and shame, overwhelming seduction by the use and abuse. The means and ways of getting and using drugs consumed my daily life. This is just a glimpse of the heaviness, the weight, the trauma of my addiction to crack cocaine, for there were many traumatic experiences in my life.

My favorite artist, *Sade*, recorded a song that I love called, *Lover's Rock*. You are the lover's rock, the rock that I cling too! Crack cocaine was my lover, and yes, I fell in love! The crack pipe smoking had me hooked, line and sinker, for many, many years. Truly, it is another world and state of existence. I was not living, but I was a dead person walking. Who could rescue me from this horrible degrading pit? Only Jesus, but God! Now my worship, my life, belongs to Jesus Christ, especially when singing those lyrics by Sade, Lover's Rock. Hear my cry!

I lived over 25 years in utter chaos and gruesome darkness, spiraling down a staircase of cocaine addiction. I had no idea it could lead to death, let alone spiritual death and bankruptcy. My desperation to live for God overcame my addiction to crack cocaine. For 25 years, the only voice I responded to was my flesh. "I want a rock right now!" In case you didn't know is cocaine in solid rock form, also known as freebasing. It became a daily, hourly obsession, always compelling me to crave, use, find, and get it by any means necessary. In the early 1970s, what had started out as social fun for partying at nightclubs, after-hour joints, and home parties become a national epidemic. Crack cocaine was rapidly spreading throughout every American city. The powder cocaine was first introduced to the rich and famous. This form of cocaine was not sniffed into one's nostrils. I fell instantly in love with it; although in previous years I experimented with top grade hash, marijuana, THC, acid, and other self-medicating drugs, this was the best. If I appear to be straightforward and transparent, I am. In many 12-step group meetings of Narcotics Anonymous and Alcohol Anonymous, one is encouraged and often compelled to become rigorously honest about their addiction. That is a necessary step in the process to recovery.

This journey inside my life as a crack addict, drug and cocaine abuser, alcoholic, sex addict, and other addictions, is not ever an easy one to share. It takes courage, and it took me years of spiritual counseling, psychotherapy, Bible study, group and individual counseling, 12-step meetings, prayers and fasting, crying, healing, regular church attendance, rigorous honesty through NA/AA meetings and sponsors and boldness to bring this story to life. It is because of the taboo about addictions and its consequences that I share this testimony, knowing that I may help someone suffering from addictions. I am concerned about those who may not know the benefits of surrendering their life to God; how to turn from walking in the flesh, how to turn from walking further into deep darkness, or how to walk in the spirit, in the light of Jesus Christ. There is total confusion, chaos, and intensified evil in the world of an active addict. A marvelous transition takes place in one's life once they surrender their life to Christ. I can testify what the Bible declares is true. I can now say, I once was spiritually blind, but now I see. I was without hope, confused, living in utter darkness, spiritually void, and without hope! Now, my life has totally changed. I am now serving as the pastor of the historic First Baptist Church in Plymouth, Massachusetts.

I know that God has a divine purpose and plan for my life. I gladly share my testimony, because I know He has a great plan for everyone who places trust in Him. I know if God was willing to deliver, save, heal, and restore the years that the devil tried to destroy, my mind, my soul, my family, my children, my relationships, my finances, my employment, my entire life and everything near and dear to me, then I am convinced that God can do it for anyone. Yes, God can! God can reach anyone, save anyone, no matter how far down in sin they have fallen. I believe that once a person surrenders their life to God through Jesus Christ, miraculous, successful, prosperous peaceful days, and a future are ahead.

In former years, when I was seeking to recover from my various addictions, I recall literally being shifted through numerous revolving doors at some of the finest detoxification centers, halfway houses, hospitals, and psychiatric wards in the state of Massachusetts. I was always crying out for help. Interestingly, I met my second husband while an inpatient at a halfway house in Boston. I learned valuable lessons about myself while there, for which I am grateful. While there, I was considered by the staff to be a model case for the halfway house. However, I did find myself oddly attracted to a man for all the wrong reasons. Nonetheless, we dated for about four months; it was not long after that we were married. Again, we both relapsed and began to use drugs together. I realized too late that I did not give heed to the warnings, "Do not enter into major decisions during the first year of your recovery." Why? Because two sick people together do not make a well person. I thought

I knew better. I can outsmart the normal statistics; show this to be. In retrospect, the temptation was toxic, and I was needy, stubborn, sick (mentally, spiritually, physically, emotionally), and relapsed. Consequently, I used for several more years, finding ways and means to get crack cocaine. My marriage became unmanageable; we separated, and I ended up back into treatment again. However, with each relapse, my use of drugs and alcohol was continually getting worse. Each time, I relapsed over and over again. It was only by the grace of God I was not found dead in some dirty crack house hallway.

As I look back over my life, it is hard to comprehend the drug addict, hustling, on-the-streets girl, I used to be. You see, I became addicted to the lifestyle of getting and using drugs. City life and the urban street scene was all so fun to me. The lights, the clubs, dressing up, weed smoking; it was an escape from life, pain, and hurt. It was an escape from the shame and guilt. The city was full of temptations that appealed to me. I was living on the edge of destruction, and I was fearless when it came to taking risks. You can only imagine the places and dark alleys, dark parks, abandoned buildings I entered or went in to use drugs, cop (buy} drugs, wherever and whenever I came up with the money. The things I did to getting money to support my habit, or to get my next hit, for over so many years, is beyond belief. The pain of guilt, shame, and remorse continued day and night. I knew it was wrong, but I just could not stop using, permanently.

There were times, for the sake of my children, I could stop temporarily. I dressed really nice, fixed my hair, wore designer clothes, heels, pumps, even worked great jobs, and I went to college. This was part of covering up how bad my addiction was getting and to make my parents feel I was okay. Those are some of the things I hid behind to disguise my addiction, and they did keep me in denial of just how bad of an addiction I had for so many years.

Although I had brief periods of sobriety, the obsessive-compulsion desire drove me again, and again to smoke crack cocaine as if my life depended on it. The truth is that it did! It owned me! I chose to numb the pain of my fluctuating, unstable emotions, and empty soul, mind, and body. I recall how, in my early 20s, I dropped down to a pant size 1. I did not see anything wrong with being so thin. I thought I looked good. For I was known to dress my tail off, to be a diva-dressing nightwalker. However, the rapid loss of weight was due to smoking crack cocaine. I was a hustler, streetwalker, street talker, liar, cheat, thief, robber, yes! Among the walking dead, the spiritual bankrupt, and hopeless. I was in denial about my using drugs and how bad things were becoming in my life. The day the lightbulb went off in my head was when I was introduced to a term I had never heard before. It was during our couple's Bible study, and the facilitator showed the parallels between when Jesus, while on the cross, was offered vinegar as a drug. He went on to explain that drug addiction comes from the Greek term pharmacia, meaning witchcraft, potions, black magic, etc.

I knew it was a matter of life and death if I returned to using drugs. My life, my mind, my soul, was in a blackout. I had mental psychosis as I was withdrawing from the cocaine. It is beyond words, the sense of urgency I felt to get all the help I needed. I realized for the first time why I was not able to stop; because I had not surrendered my life to Jesus. I felt a sense of release from the pressure of blaming myself for messing up not only my life, but also the lives of all those who loved and cared about me. Mainly, my Christian mother, and the two children that needed their birth mother in their life. I did not know who I was anymore, and the damage to my heart, mind, and soul is just unthinkable. I could have been institutionalized for all the crazy, evil, and deranged things I thought, as well as those I committed during my active addiction.

After being sober for a year, and sponsoring women while participating in the AA, 12-step group meetings in the city of Brockton, Massachusetts, I was introduced to a staff-servant leader of Mount Moriah Baptist Church. He provided me, along with my estranged husband, marriage counseling to restore our broken relationship. For the first time in my life, I had a ray of hope. I came to believe that our marriage could be saved in spite of our infidelity, addictions, resentments, and forgiveness. During the sessions, I learned that our history did not have the final word about our destiny! What God did for me, through those words of wise counsel, was greater than what my family, friends, colleagues, medical doctors, psychiatrists, and caseworkers could ever do or imagine. In the process of reconciliation, we both were led to accept Jesus Christ as our savior, and the word of God became the foundation for rearranging our priorities. I learned, and came to believe, that God can and still does perform miracles!

I made a firm commitment to stay in the house of the

Lord. I desperately needed the Lord. I wanted to learn, hear, breathe, and to consistently study the word of God and be a doer of His word. That is what gave me the inner assurance that my broken life was being healed. One evening at Bible study, I received a rhema word from the Lord, which Jesus came to set the captives free! That word was especially for me! I am a living witness! I was set free to live for Christ! Glory to God, I'm sober and I'm free! Yes, God can do anything! What God did for me; God can do for anyone!

Testimony of
Kristin Cox
Florida
Recovery & Restoration

Therefore, if any man be in Christ,
he is a new creature: old things are passed away;
behold, all things are become new.

2 Corinthians 5:17

My name is Kristin Cox. I was blessed to have been born and raised by godly parents who loved and faithfully served the Lord. Parents who expressed unconditional love for me. Sometimes, because my parents were the youth pastors in my home church, I found myself in church prayer meetings and worship services all day long (starting at 7 a.m. and lasting until late evening). For a while, my life consisted of church, church, church, and more church. It was all right with me, because I enjoyed watching people be healed, delivered, and set free in the name of Jesus Christ. I was taught by my parents to find God for myself, and when I did, to always love Him with all of my heart, mind, and soul. This I did! In my search for God, I also was finding something else about myself. I had a heart of compassion for all people, especially the less fortunate and the lost.

I recall, during school days, I found myself witnessing to classmates so often that my teachers informed my parents; and when I got home, they sat me down and told me that I was sent to school to learn not to preach. They also encouraged me to know there was a time and place when the Gospel could be more appropriately shared. I recall one Sunday when the pastor invited all of the children and youth to the altar to question us about Jesus Christ. I remember how often I got in trouble with my dad, because I was always the first person to raise my hand and never gave others a chance to answer the questions. I just could not help myself! It was always an exhilarating moment for me when anyone asked for someone to say something about Jesus. I was always ready! My dad would often get angry with me because I was always the first one to jump up with a comment. The pastor later spoke to my dad and told him not to be too hard on me. He realized that God was stirring something He had deeply embedded within me that was my destiny.

In my mind's eye, I can still envision images of

glistening water as it sparkled so radiantly, as if the heavens had opened to rain down thousands of diamonds into my church's baptismal pool. I was eight years old, being baptized for the first time. I heard the pastor declare over my head, "Brother Kristin, on the profession of your faith in Jesus Christ, I now baptize you in the name of the Father, the Son and the Holy Spirit." Immediately, I was submerged into the warm waters. I had never been so excited. I felt as though everything changed and I would never be the same. I still remember the smiles on the face of my parents and the church's elder saints. I remember the warm embraces of acceptance into the family of God. Because I was only an eight-year-old boy, I was not aware until many years later that there was an invisible, yet very adversarial force, that was aggressively working out a strategic plan to tempt me to curse God, live any way I chose, but without hope.

When I was adolescent, I can recall the special moments when my dad used to anoint my head with blessed oil. There were times when he was constantly anointing me for almost everything. So much olive oil was poured on me that I began to think our family might have stocks and bonds with the Pompeian Organic Oil

Company. Our family went through a least one bottle every month; that's a lot of anointing! Those anointing moments blessed me, because even at this early age, my life was filled with a deeper passion for the righteous things of God.

I also began to experience the intrusive forces of the adversary of my soul. Those attacks caused me to question what I believed about Jesus Christ, and what I believed about myself.

Jesus is the healer, the way maker, and the only true deliverer of our soul. These eternal truths were spiritual seeds sown early into my life and truths, which continue to shape the man that I am today. As I began my walk of faith, those beliefs came into question. I remained active in school and did very well; also, I continued to be very active in my church. Overall, I was feeling good, because I began to experience the hand of God moving over my life. He was blessing me with favor. I experienced God doing for me what the old saints in my church testified to during prayer meetings. "God made a way out of no way." Everything in my life was going fine. In school, I was an up-and-coming baseball star; I played first chair tenor saxophone in the school jazz band, and I was an honor roll student. In church, I was knowledgeable of the Bible and continued to share the Gospel with my peers and others.

In the year 2000, it is as though everything in my life changed. The invisible adversary of my soul turned my life upside down and proceeded to tempt me to curse God and die. I was still an adolescent, only 13 years old. One day my mom informed us that she was having unusual stomach pains. From my perspective, it was no big deal, nothing that a tablespoon of Pepto-Bismol, magnesium citrate, and a heartfelt prayer couldn't cure. That was not the case. We eventually took my mother to the hospital, only to be told the devastating news, "She has stage four colon cancer." At that moment, my faith was greatly tested and pressed to the breaking point.

That evening, out of desperation and fervent prayer, I made a covenantal arrangement with God. On bended knees and folded hands, with tears flowing down my eyes, I prayed for my mother. As a 13-year-old teenager, I prayed the only words that came to my mind. I earnestly prayed, "Okay, God, it's me, your son Kristin. I know I'm not perfect, and I'm sorry for everything that I have ever done wrong, and I promise from this day forward that if you heal my mother, I will never turn away from you. I promise to serve you until you call me home." After that prayer, which I believed to be a binding covenant, I rose up feeling a sense of peace and spiritual confidence. I honestly believed that God heard my prayer, and because I knew he loved our family; He was sure to answer with a miracle. I knew that God had my back on this one!

All the sermons I heard about miraculous healings and deliverances; it was now my turn to believe it would become a present reality for my mother. I felt that it was now my turn to be a recipient of the faith seeds we had sown. It was now my turn to touch the hem of Jesus' garment on my mother's behalf so that she might be made whole. It was my turn to dip six times into the Jordan River, and on the seventh time, she would be made whole. As my mother's proxy, it was now my turn to be carried to the pool at Bethesda and step into the troubled waters, and she would be made whole. It was now my time to watch God "make a way out of no way." God would do the miraculous, and my mother would be made completely well again.

Well, things did not turn out as I expected. My mother became sicker as the days passed. She gradually began to lose her hair and a lot of weight. To my amazement, she never lost her faith in God. It was as though each day, despite her affliction, her faith was renewed. At the time, I did not realize that God was doing a new thing in her life. I was so caught up in my own pain. At that age, I did not understand why I could not stand as her proxy, to have her pain and suffering taken away. Nonetheless, in my pain, I began to doubt if God really heard my prayer. I wondered if God was mad at me or was so disappointed in me that He refused to answer me. I questioned myself and doubted if I really had enough faith to believe a miracle would happen. I was tempted to reject the existence of a living or loving God. I slipped into a dark place. I started thinking; maybe God really did place a curse on my family. It might be there because of something my father or mother or a distant relative had done in the past, or it just might be punishment for things that I did or failed to do. Could this be a generational curse? All those thoughts flooded into my mind.

Consequently, as the days passed by, it was so hard for me to watch my mother slowly deteriorate from the cancer. A day came when I no longer had the strength to visit her in the hospital. My pain was so unbearable, I couldn't even talk to her on the phone. That was my momma, the woman who nurtured me, who taught me how to tie my shoes, who saved me from many whippings, who acknowledged my birthdays with parties. She was the one who taught me so much about Jesus. To imagine that I couldn't bear to face the reality of her dying, even today, elicits tears of sorrow.

Exactly one year later, April 2001, on Resurrection Sunday, while standing at a pew in the back of the church worshiping with the congregation, I felt a gentle wind flow past me. Right then I sensed that it was the spirit of my mother. She had departed to be with the Lord. This was confirmed as soon as we got home from church. We walked into the house and the phone rang. It was the official word that my mother had passed. What I felt at that moment, words could not express. It was as though a knife pierced deep into my heart and was radically pulled out. At that moment everything that I was taught; everything that had encouraged me, persuaded me, or inspired me; everything that my sense of identity or purpose rested upon, at that very moment, became empty and meaningless. My mother died, and now my life was shattered.

I felt betrayed by God. He failed me. Suddenly my faith walk was an unreal and fictitious lie. As the days, month, and years passed, because I believed that God no longer loved me, and because I doubted the teachings of the Bible, I felt shattered just like the nursery character, Humpty Dumpty. If you happen to remember the story: Humpty Dumpty sat on the wall. Humpty Dumpty had a great fall. All the kings' horses and all the kings' men couldn't put Humpty Dumpty back together again.

At the most vulnerable point in my life, Satan threw his fiery darts at me, tempting me to turn my back of God, to devalue my sense of worth by embracing the lies and sinful practices of the world. I started living as I chose without any regard for the consequences. Unknowingly, I became drunk with the wine of the world, all the while I was desperately searching for love, acceptance. Something that would heal my broken spirit and now sin sick soul, but I was searching in all the wrong places. I listened to all types of contemporary rap music. I tried all kinds of drugs. I partied, I drank, and I participated in all manner of dangerous activities. I even joined a gang hoping to find acceptance, even though I knew many of them were broken, confused, angry, and hurting people, just like me. I eventually developed a severe addiction that thrust me into a dishonorable lifestyle. That lifestyle led me to prison. I was convicted of a felony and sentenced to 15 years in prison. My spirit became cold and bitter, and my heart always remained broken. While in prison I often felt alone and forsaken. I had nobody! Let me take that back. The only one who stuck faithfully by my side throughout the ordeal was the very one I rebelled against at the passing of my mother; that was my dad. In my darkest moments, I had no idea that God by His grace was restoring my relationship with my dad, reconciling me back to Himself and working everything out for my good. I really wanted to be reconciled to God, but I still had to overcome my anger and trust issues with Him. Emotionally, I knew that I did not want to go back to the lifestyle that got me confined to prison. I surmised that I needed another heart-to-heart conversation with God. In my arrogance, I convinced myself that I had to tell God how I honestly felt. This is simply what I told God.

God, I'm angry, I'm bitter, I'm offended because you didn't heal my mother. She died, and you broke my heart into millions of pieces. God could have ignored me because of my arrogance, but He didn't. Instead, He opened the eyes of my understanding by leading me back to the Holy Scriptures. There, God corrected my thinking, and helped me to understand that the life of my mother was always under His loving care. Her death, like the death of all of God's children is precious in His sight. Most importantly, He helped me understand that death is not the end of life; for a believer in Christ, it is the glorious transition point into eternal life. That revelation gave me peace and healed my wandering sin-sick soul. Then, God showed me how much He loved me. I was sentenced to 15 years, but God brought me out in eight!

Now my life is renewed. I am a new creation in Christ Jesus. I have a peace that surpasses all understanding. I am truly blessed. I have am released from prison: I am reunited with my father; I completed school and earned a B.A. degree in religious education, and I am now working toward a second degree in nouthetic counseling. I am married to a beautiful Christian woman, Marjorie Cox. We have two daughters, Khaliyah, nine years old, Kaylee, nine months, and a son on the way. I have a super job. Moreover, we recently were blessed by God to purchase a new home for our family. I love the Lord! My life will never be the same! I am set free! I have come too far to turn back now! To God be the glory for the great things He has done!

Testimony of
Phyllis I. Brown
Massachusetts
Great Favor

Thy word have I hid in my heart,
that I might not sin against Thee.

Psalm 119: 11

I really do not know where to begin. It seems as far back as memory takes me; I have always known Jesus loves me! In fact, one of my most favorite hymns is Jesus Loves Me This I Know. For me, there is an on-going deep desire, a real yearning to know more about Jesus and God.

As a preteen, I enrolled in The Radio Bible Class; for a good number of years, I would complete and send off the lessons that they corrected and returned. I, along with four of my siblings, sang in the chancel choir. I can remember the choir director telling us not to just give lip service to what we sang, but to give meaning to the words while singing them. I slowly began to pay closer attention to the lyrics of the different hymns and anthems. In so doing, I began to visualize and understand God's goodness, His mercy, and His grace. This also drew me deeper into the Bible, as I found most of the anthems we sang came directly from the Bible. I officially gave my life to Christ at the church of my youth shortly after turning 12 and rededicated my life to Christ Jesus at the age of 52!

During that 40-year span, a lot of life happened. Throughout the early years of parenting, my church attendance began to dwindle from an every-Sunday occurrence to intermittent, then sporadic at best. At the age of 17, I graduated from high school on June 2, 1952. I married in 1954 and was blessed with the birth of four children (between December of 1957 and September of 1961); separated in November of 1963 and divorced in 1973 (after many attempts to salvage my marriage).

The first Tuesday in November (Election Day, 1963), my then-husband went to work at 6 a.m. and did not come home, or call, until New Year's Eve, when he came home about 10 p.m. to pick up some of his clothes. As he told my then pastor, he just got tired of it all and left. As he was going through his closet to get clothes suitable for a New Year's Eve party, I decided to leave the house. I figured if I could be struck by a car (or better, cars), my children would be better off being raised by their father.

I really did not think I, a hearing-impaired mother, could sufficiently raise my children without their father in the home as well. I walked the streets at almost midnight on December 31, 1963, against traffic signals and directly into the flow of moving traffic, yet, nothing would hit me ... I did not know what to do.

I thought because of the holiday, it would be so simple to be hit by a driver or two. I thought of going to my church (we always celebrated Watch Night Services), but I knew those present would leave there soon, and I didn't want anyone knowing what was happening in my life, or what I tried to do to eliminate the problem. I decided to go to the pastor's home and sit on the back steps until they arrived. After a short time, I saw the headlights as cars pulled into the driveway. Unfortunately, they brought others home with them! Not being able to think of another alternative and being very cold, I eventually knocked on the back door. Pastor answered, and, unseen by others, escorted me to his study. I remember one of the first questions I asked Pastor (when meeting him for the first time, as he answered the call to pastor my church), concerned his belief regarding confidentiality; if he sanctioned the confidence of his conversations with parishioners. He responded positively. Now, on this night, I needed assurance of one more thing; my question to him that night was: Would God have forgiven me if I had taken my own life? He responded: Yes, He would have. I was so relieved, my floodgates opened! Now it was too late, I had revealed my plan and could not now carry it out. After a time of sharing, counseling, and making sure I was able to be alone, Pastor took me home. He asked my husband if he would remain there overnight, stating he would return some time during the late morning hours the following day. My husband did stay through the night, leaving prior to pastor's arrival.

In 1964, my children and I began consistent attendance in both Sunday school and church, and I slowly re-involved myself in several ministries. However, in no uncertain terms did my love and trust in God through His son, Christ Jesus, ever become displaced. He has always been and continues to be the one I turn to for guidance and direction through good times and the not so good times, because I know His eye is on the sparrow (and I know he watches me)! Also, during this time, although I was born the eighth child in a family of eight girls and three boys, in His plan for my life God brought a second family into the lives of my children and myself. This "kinship" has flourished for more than 50 years and encompasses the entire family of sisters, brothers, aunts, uncles, cousins, nieces, and nephews. God is truly able to do more than we can ever imagine!

The third family God tucked me safely into is the church home that became mine when, in 1988, I rededicated my life to Christ and was baptized by immersion. God has blessed me immeasurably. Especially through couples within this church, even though I am a single person. I received my first car from one couple, and another couple (several years later and with the financial help of others within the church family) secured a second car for me when the carriage simply fell to the ground while I was driving it! One of these two couples repeatedly took me to dinner for many years after morning service at least 40 times each year – that is beyond blessing! God has continually showered me with great favor all the years of my life. The greatest favor of all is the knowing that God loves me unconditionally, just as I am, in spite of any of my actions. That God loves me whether I have been good or bad, indifferent or basking in His presence, joyful or mournful, lovable or unlovable, obedient or disobedient, a truth-teller or a liar. I could go on and on, but you know what I'm talking about. He kept my hand in His and carried me when I was faint, worn out, or unable to function through the trials and hard times of my life, hanging on by only a thread, wanting to give-up, and not hold on.

I am more than thankful! I trust my Heavenly Father with every fiber of my total being. Early in my life, God showered me with so many blessings. If I had the gift of a thousand tongues, they still could not adequately express the depth of my trust and love for my Heavenly Father.

There are two ministries that overshadow the other gifts that I possess, and I know they are special blessings from my Father in Heaven ... they are the gift of ministry to children and the ministry of hospitality. This gift of ministry to children began at a very early age on the street I lived on. One day, I noticed a little girl playing along the side of her house all by herself. I noticed that she was always alone, playing by herself. I received permission from my mother to knock on her door and introduce myself to her parents (I was not to go into the home) and ask if it was all right for me to play with the child who was about three or four years of age (I was nine). This friendship with the child and her family continued for several years, and my younger sister and I were invited to vacation with them in Duxbury for several weeks during many summers.

As a teenager, I taught in the church school, either kindergarten or first grade children. When my own children began Sunday school, I returned to teaching this same age group, and continued to teach all the years my children were enrolled and beyond. I was asked to serve on the diaconate at my present church, and one of the duties is to teach the church school. I have taught both kindergarten/first grade and the baptismal class for children. I took on the responsibility as the director of the church-based after school program, and God allowed me to reach the whole child; those He called unto Himself ... what a privilege! They complained that I was mean, but when I see them in today's world, they thank me for being there for them, not only academically, but spiritually as well. Nevertheless, that was God's plan for their lives and mine – in spite of my hearing loss, God used me to teach and to reach His children. I gained so much simply being in their lives, not just respect, but a mutual love from them and their parents, and a genuine spiritual kinship. In spite of my hearing loss, God allowed me to touch the lives and hearts of His children, and for that, I am most grateful.

I was surprised when someone told me I was a good

listener. I marveled at that and I thought, here I am, unable to hear, and I am being told I am a good listener? Then, God helped me understand that listening requires more than just hearing, but is the ability to be present for another in such a way that you fully comprehend what they are saying, and do so without interrupting. That is a God-given talent.

The admonitions of the Apostle Paul in Ephesians 5:19 and life in general has also taught me that hymns and spiritual songs are a great anecdote for the soul. At a young age, hymns often provided me great solace, especially when I felt I had been wronged, taken advantage of, and even lied about. With great gusto, I often sang Farther Along We'll Know All About It, believing God would punish those people who continually hurt me. After all, I was His, and this song gave me the ability to get through it. Nevertheless, as I began to mature – not only in age, but also in my growing in Christ, I relinquished my preconceived notions and allowed God to teach me. I no longer needed God to take revenge on others for me. As I grew closer to Him, and began to know more about Him, He began to give me a clearer and better understanding and knowledge of Himself and increased my healing as I learned the art of forgiveness and trust.

And God walks with me and He talks with me, and He tells me I am His own.... I know to whom much is given, much is required. I do thoroughly enjoy my life in Christ, and I pray it never, ever changes, except to grow stronger, deeper, and more intimate. I pray that as I continue to grow, I may consistently show others the Christ in me... that they, too, may be free! I can truly say that I do not worry about anything, nor am I bound by fear. Praise the Lord!

One morning, during a Sunday worship service in the early 80s, God unveiled to me just how free in Christ I really am, and I was inspired to write these few words:

I am free, I am free! Jesus has liberated me.

He took me by the hand; He released the elastic band.

And I am free, indeed!

Eighty-two years ago, March 8, 1935, a baby girl was born; the eighth child (seventh girl) of her parents, Charles Lynwood, Sr. and E. Louise Smith. Unbeknownst at that time to her parents, this child was born with a congenital nerve loss, resulting in a progressive deterioration of hearing. When my parents learned of this condition, they didn't tell me, because they did not want me to be stigmatized and labeled as handicapped; and as a result,

I thought that everyone was like me and when engrossed in what they were doing, they did not always hear what was going on around them. Through the years, I picked up' lip-reading on my own. It was not until the birth of my first child, at the age of 22, that I began to realize I didn't hear well.

After going through new audiology testing with doctors at Massachusetts Eye and Ear Infirmary, retrieving my records going back 40-some years, I learned the news of my birth defect and was fitted for a hearing aid. Then, I began to understand some things I experienced in earlier years were all because I did not hear, and had nothing to do with my ability to function, my intelligence, nor the person that I am. Many people classified me as being stuck up; walking around with my nose in the air; thinking I was so much better than they were (because I didn't laugh at their jokes, etc.). While I was going to Sunday night Young People's Fellowship, a young man interning at the church as part of his training for the ministry had all the youth participate in some type of mental testing exercise. My mother later shared with me that in his report he stated I was suffering some type of learning or mental disability, which made it difficult for me to follow directions, verbalize, share in a group setting, or even complete a paper within a given period! When in reality, I probably did not hear the questions we were supposed to answer, nor the instructions on how to complete them. Yet, the reports from the three schools I attended (elementary, junior high, and senior sigh) always showed me to be an honor roll student, one never absent nor tardy from first grade to high school graduation at age 17. When my oldest brother died several years ago, a childhood acquaintance told me most of them talked about how stuck-up I was; she said I never responded to any of them as we passed on the street or in school.

In 2014, while visiting family at Thanksgiving, I dropped my hearing aid, and when I returned home, I learned it was damaged beyond repair. The audiologist recommended that I return to Massachusetts Eye and Ear to see if I would qualify for the cochlear implant. I believe that period (between 2015 and 2017) was the hardest for me in coping with my inability to hear. My hearing, itself, was at its lowest ebb, probably because I did not have an aid during that time. I was suffering from profound hearing loss and becoming increasingly distressed as I attended meetings and events that required hearing. Although I had been deemed a qualifying candidate, it took the insurance companies nearly two full years to give approval for their portion of the cost.

On March 30, 2017, I underwent elected surgery which the doctors said would restore more than 30 years of lost hearing. Before the surgery, I knew when the phone was ringing, because all the phones lit up with each incoming call. However, the glorious moment for me happened in church the first time I wore the implant on a Sunday morning! Before, every time a gentleman played the sax, I had to ask someone: What is he playing? However, on that morning, I wanted to get up and shout! I could not only hear the sax; I knew he was playing How Great Thou Art! Tears of pure joy and thanksgiving streamed down my cheeks, I heard the sax from the very beginning, and understood what I was listening to. Thank you, Jesus!

My heart is filled with thanksgiving to God. He allows me to ask questions and even bombard Him with my facts (like He didn't already know – mostly when I don't want to do what His Holy Spirit is encouraging me to do, or when I am trying to have my own way, and I remember full well when I did that for almost a whole year).

Dear Lord, when I finally yielded my own stubborn will to yours, when I was finally obedient to the prompting of your Holy Spirit within me, that's when you gave me total peace; your peace that knows no bounds! That peace which gives one the ability to sing and dance even while going through!

You know who God is, but there is still so much more to learn. I have a peace within me that nothing and no one can change. Yes, I go through difficult and hard moments, and it can be terribly hard to get through those, but this I know – God is always by my side; I am never alone! Because God has given me His understanding and His wisdom, I no longer go through anything alone. In addition, I have a peace within me that nothing can change.

Thank you, Lord God, for keeping me, and teaching me, and guiding me, and protecting me, and preparing for me. For allowing me to see your hand in every area of my life, even while I was in my mother's womb. You see, even before I was born, God was preparing for my birth into the family He chose as mine. My mother taught my older siblings how to communicate with each other. She instructed them not shout at each other from room to room; but to stop their tasks for a few moments and go to the room of the individual they wished to speak with, have the conversation, and then return to their task. Only God! How could my parents have known one of their babies would be born with a hearing disability?

I thank you, Lord God, for choosing me despite my weaknesses, my procrastinations, my faults, and my failures. Thank you, Father, for not giving up on me, even when I strayed a far distance away from you. I am most thankful that you did not turn your back on me! I am thankful, precious Lord, that you looked beyond my faults and saw my need and continue to hold my hand and lead me on. Thank you, Lord, for loving me and not condemning me. Thank you for the gift of life.

I would not change, even if I could, any part of my past, because everything has helped make me who I am today. I know that the Lord has used all that has happened as part of my learning experience. It is He who led me through it all, who taught me how my disobedience took me down paths I would not have endured was I not been impatient, and waited for the Holy Spirit's leading. Thank you for teaching me to be forgiving, to be truthful, to be loving, and to be kind.

Worship the Lord in the Beauty of Holiness . . .

Bow down before Him,

His praises proclaim!

For Your ministrations to me every day of my life;

For truly being my Friend above all friends;

My Father, He who watches over me,

Protecting me as no other can;

He who breathes life into me

That I may have the strength to continue

When the going gets rough and the pathway

is not clear;

Thank you, for favor;

Thank you, for blessing me;

Hallelujah! Hallelujah! Hallelujah!

Testimony of
Kecia Lopes
Maryland
The Cost Of Carrying The Cross

But in a great house there are not only vessels of
gold and of silver, but also of wood and of earth;
and some to honour, and some to dishonour.
If a man therefore purges himself from these,
he shall be a vessel unto honour, sanctified,
and meet for the master's use,
and prepared unto every good work.

2 Timothy 2:20-21

As ministers of the Gospel, we are inspired to write and develop sermons. However, the truth of the matter is we become and live a sermon each day that speaks to a watching world. Our lives are constantly in the Potter's hand for honorable or dishonorable use.

A surrendered heart and sacrificial life for God's purpose is a crucial component of our testimony for others. We can talk about giving good testimony, but are we willing to endure and go through what it takes to get that testimony? We are set apart for the unexpected turns, challenges, and unknowns that take form in our lives. Jesus says that some honor Him with their lips, but their hearts are far from Him (Mark 7: 7). I can testify to what that entails.

As I began my journey as a Christian, it was evident early on that there were many things I had no clue about. For example, I performed religious acts of service and ignored building the personal relationship. I could teach, sing in the choir, and work on planning committees to conduct conferences and events, but neglected establishing a true and intimate relationship with the Father.

I always had a heart for God and His people, and loved doing the church thing, but I never knew or understood why God required more of me. As my Christian life evolved, I realized something was missing. I felt at times like I was going through the motions, but not experiencing the full joy and power that I knew existed in Jesus Christ.

I was born and raised in Dorchester, Massachusetts, the oldest girl of three siblings. I am have four children and five grandchildren. I have been married for over 21 years and worked in the private, public, and nonprofit sectors. I first accepted Christ in 1975 and was baptized in the Ohatchee River at the First Baptist Church of Ohatchee, Alabama. From the age of five, I would spend the summer months with Bigmama (my spiritual grandmother), who lived in Alabama. She visited our family in Massachusetts during springtime, and then took me back with her to Alabama for the summer. Since that time, the hand of the Lord has always been upon me. He has protected and guided me through many trials and tribulations. My life journey consisted of experiences involving physical and emotional abuse, homelessness, abandonment, divorce, housing discrimination, two near-death experiences, dead-end relationships, teenage pregnancy, and many other unfortunate encounters and afflictions. Only by the grace of God did I made it through.

If the Lord had not been on my side, I do not know where I would be right now. I believe every positive and negative encounter that took place was preparation for my service to God.

At 17, I became pregnant with my first child. It was a challenging and difficult time in my life because I was put out of my parents' home and became a product of the foster care system. Even though the circumstances were difficult, my foster mother was a kind, but strict, woman. Mr. and Mrs. Fielder were in their early 60s, and they opened their home to foster children. I was the oldest of four at that time, and pregnant with my first son. This placement was supposedly temporary until another placement could be found; but because I was pregnant, I ended up staying with the Fielder's until giving birth to my son.

In the seventh month of my pregnancy, I went to the hospital because I felt ill and was vomiting excessively. When I reached the hospital, I was rushed into the emergency room, because my appendix was leaking bile inside of my body. As soon as the doctors opened me up to perform surgery, my appendix ruptured. It was only by God's grace, mercy, and protection that neither my son nor myself died during this life-threatening ordeal. The doctors said if my appendix had burst before reaching the hospital, both of us would have died. The miracle in all of this was that both of our lives were spared; my son was unaffected by the surgery, and he remained intact for another two and one-half months so I was able to deliver him at full term.

I have undergone many transitional phases to become a humble servant for God. Another trying and difficult time in my life was in 1994, when I went through a horrific divorce due to my husband's unfaithfulness. The betrayal, emotional distress, and lack of financial support led me toward bitter feelings of anger and resentment. I wanted my ex-husband to suffer for what he did to me, because I felt he was responsible for our shattered family. The pain from the adulterous affair was overwhelming, causing me severe bouts of depression. I was despondent and hopeless, which led me to contemplate suicidal thoughts. I could not see my way out, nor how to move forward, until one day, the Lord led my mother to tell me to start praying and reading the Bible. At that point, I prayed to God and asked Him to take away the pain, hurt, and bad feelings, and replace them with something else. To my surprise, God answered by taking the pain away and beginning the healing and filling my heart with His love. In addition, within three days, God sent my current husband.

In 1996, I remarried and rededicated my life completely to Jesus Christ. At this point, I learned about the administration aspect of the church, but did not fully embrace the relational component of having a personal relationship with God. Joining Mount Moriah Baptist Church and attending Bible studies, conferences, and retreats, I learned the value of reading the Bible, praying, and fasting. Through this process, I began to grow spiritually and teach the word of God. Initially, I taught children in Sunday school, then proceeded to conduct Bible studies in my home, and eventually progressed to teaching and ministering to men and women at the Dartmouth House of Correction. This level of training and preparation opened the door to God's call on my life.

Our experiences become either a hindrance or a reference point for how to do things differently. In making the right choices to move forward, the goal is not to make the same mistakes, learn from previous mistakes made, and use biblical principles as a guide. Maintaining a personal relationship with God is essential so that we do not forget His ways, His word, His instructions, and His commandments. God's word must always remain in our hearts, so that we do not abandon His ways.

In 2011, I became a licensed minister to preach the word of God. Answering the call of God for my life brought on a new dimension of testing and challenges. These challenges are predestined for God's purpose. The word says, I became a minister according to the stewardship from God, which was given to me for you to fulfill the word of God. (Colossians 1: 25).

Each element of testing revealed more of my need to draw closer to God. This level of responsibility and accountability to God initiated humility, persecution, afflictions, sacrifice, long suffering, holiness, consecration, and sanctification in my life. However, I am encouraged because the word says: God has saved and called us with a holy calling, not according to works, but according to His own purpose and grace that was given to us in Christ Jesus before time began. (2 Timothy 8-9).

The call of God has a cost associated with it. The cost is astronomical, and influences relationships of family and friends, personal dreams and aspirations, security, and livelihood, forfeiting everything to follow Christ. Scripture states When He had called the people to Himself, with His disciples also, He said to them, "Whoever desires to come after Me, let him deny himself, and take up his cross, and follow Me. For whoever desires to save his life will lose it, but whoever loses his life for My sake and the Gospel's will save it. For what will it profit a man if he gains the whole world and loses his soul. (Mark 8: 34-36).

This passage of scripture emphasizes the importance and true meaning of carrying the cross in preparation for ministry. There is a process necessary to continually walk out your call for ministry and maintain a relationship with God. The backdrop of being saved and walking with God comes at a cost, and you must be willing to carry that cross.

There are four things I want to share about accepting the call to ministry:

- The call requires us to be set apart for God's use;

- The call requires us to live holy because God is holy;

- The call requires a surrendered heart that corresponds to a surrendered life, and;

- The call requires being sacrificial in everything as a pleasing aroma and contribution to God's work on the earth.

Everyone's call is different. It depends on your individual relationship with God. Some are on the frontline, and some are in the back office. In either regard, everyone's cross is different. You need to know who you are in that equation. Are you front line or back office?

For me, service to God means this: God wants me to know, beyond a shadow of a doubt, that He chose me, He loves me; and I must fight the good fight of faith that trusts His word at all costs and maintains a sacrificial life, a surrendered heart and use, regardless of the situations that come my way. God knows my destiny. He promised never to forget me or leave me alone. God is in complete control of my life. Everything comes from Him. He is the one orchestrating and ordering my footsteps. The key is that I continue to learn how to be content where God has led me, and God intends to use me for His glory, and for my spiritual growth and development.

Moreover, for each of us, our decisions to obey and follow are based securely upon biblical principles and priorities. As we live for God, we must examine and identify what we are doing, and why we are doing, a thing. It is through this process we discover our true motive and the intent of our heart, and whether or not it aligns with God's will and purpose for our lives. Reading God's word daily keeps our heart moldable and our spirit alive for spiritual development. Studying the word on a weekly basis prepares us for service to God, and a word to share with others who need encouragement. In this way, we are a vessel in the hands of the potter, to bring Him glory as we serve His people.

It is a blessing to know that God has given us His son Jesus as an example to follow when we go through various trials and attacks from the enemy. Jesus counteracted the enemy's plot to tempt Him to abandon and stray away from God and to serve the idols of this world with the word. As Jesus was able to speak the word of God against the enemy, we can do the same to overcome traps, temptations, and tactics of the adversary. Jesus fasted for 40 days and 40 nights and was prepared for the enemy's attack. He lived a life of holiness, consecration, and sanctification, and was set apart for the Father's use because He was righteous before God.

As we face life challenges and difficulties, our first level of defense is to draw closer to God, praise Him for the issues we are facing, and believe that He will intervene on our behalf and bring us through to the other side. We are not in control; He is, and we must allow God to get the glory for His will, purpose, and plan to be fulfilled in our life. Because the scripture says: And let us not grow weary while doing good, for in due season we shall reap if we do not lose heart. (Galatians 6: 9).

Discovery of who you are in the Lord reveals over

time who you are in the kingdom of God. It comes from your previous life, before you were saved. But now God is anointing what you were doing in the natural realm for His service in the spiritual realm.

The key point is: an intimate relationship with God is true service – love the Lord and love thy neighbor; this is true service.

Testimony of
Dr. Marcietta (Wilson) Coleman
Ohio
My New Self

And we know that in all things God works
for the good of those who love him,
who have been called according to his purpose.

Romans 8: 28

A m I ready, do I have faith in the process of science? Does placing trust in the process of science mean that I do not have faith in God? Interesting thing about life – what I frequently tell my patients about my faith is that if you love God, and have faith in His ability, you will come to understand and know that God can use anything and anybody to effectuate your healing. Healing is not some tablet on Mount Sinai; it can be medicine. Nearly six months out of the hospital, I truly appreciate my life, and the ability to comb my hair, cut cabbage, and exercise. I am very thankful for the people and technologies that aided me in getting to this place. And I know these people were all God sent.

I consider myself neither brave nor heroic. I failed

to make real pressing sacrifices in life until after age 40 because of fear. Fear of rejection, of not being pretty enough, tall enough, smart enough, or loud enough. I have always been sure of my abilities. Things that I can control, i.e., who I love, where I go to school, how far I go in my education, and where I work. I never liked things where someone else gets to decide for me regardless of my merit. I like control. The only thing I have surrendered to is God. I truly believe this journey is about my trust of others and how to be vulnerable and exposed.

When I was a senior in college, my mother was diagnosed with breast cancer. Now, more than 25 years later, I faced screenings that showed I carry positive markers for breast cancer. I opted to have a prophylactic mastectomy. So, not bravery, but close surveillance and praying for early detection, isn't my idea of fun. I have two young boys and a husband. I want to get old; I want to see my grandchildren; I want to travel, retire, and sleep in late. I don't want breast cancer. I will die someday, but I prefer it not be from something I could prevent.

I was offered close observation and the ability to have an MRI every six months. I just could not imagine having to test and wait. It's not my style; it's not controlling enough. When I met with the geneticist, he asked me to tell the plastic surgeon whenever I was ready, and the general surgeon seemed perplexed as to why I was so definitive at my age. She didn't know who I was; she didn't know I never had a love affair with my breasts. She never knew I didn't think I was strong enough to handle cancer. She didn't know I was prepared to say yes since 1992.

I am from a small nuclear family. My grandfather was born in 1897 and was the youngest boy of 11 kids. He moved to Cleveland, Ohio, after a few years in college and service in WW1 and met my grandmother. After 15 years of marriage, they finally conceived, first, my aunt, then my mom and her twin (who was stillborn). Many of their relatives died or were lost prior to my birth and maturation, so our history is limited.

My mother's mom also died when she was 16, so the traditional person to pass on information was no longer alive. Her secrets were forever lost. My mother's cancer was seen as a fluke; but later, her sister developed breast cancer in her 60s, and my aunt's daughter developed thyroid cancer. This prompted me to be proactive. My kids were aware of our family history and encouraged me to be tested. Unlike when my mom was diagnosed, and I was not told until I came home for summer break;

my kids were there.

During my medical training and career, I knew there was genetic testing available; however, it wasn't until Christmas 2016 that I put fear behind and decided whatever the outcome, God had me covered. After my MRI, it was clear I could not do this again and again. It was too long, uncomfortable, and when the contrast went in, I didn't like that feeling. This was not for me. So, my surgery was set July 28, 2017.

I am a person who believes that what is for me is mine and no one else's, and the only way not to have what God has promised me is to fail to do the work or preparation. Before my surgery, I knew I was going to be okay no matter what because it was God's plan. My fear wasn't of the surgery, but of my recovery and the new body I must become comfortable in. I also was afraid about how supportive my spouse would be. This would take him out of his comfort zone, and I feared I would resent him in the end due to his lack of compassion. But in the end, I had to keep going back to my purpose in life; the service I believed I was called to do, and the mother I was charged with being. So, whatever obstacle came my way; I had the goods to do it, because I had to. God knew I longed for home, so he placed moving to Cleveland in my husband's heart. He knew I would need help, so he made sure my friend's house was ready for recovery, and there was space for my mommy to help. All the pieces were in place.

We arrived for surgery, and I changed and got my IV, telling jokes all the while. I never remembered going to sleep or waking. This was my prayer to God, and he answered. When I got to my room and was conscious, my pain was zero on the right, but eight (out of 10) on the left, and this remained through the night. By the morning I did my own examination, and found I had swelling, which was later confirmed as a hematoma. I had to go back to the operating room. These postop hematomas can cause death due to large amounts of blood loss or difficulty finding the bleeder; however, God was merciful. I was fine and discharged the next day. In three weeks, I was back to work, moving slowly, but back. And now, six months out, I am still so fortunate and blessed. I will have my exchange surgery in February and finally will be able to sleep on my stomach again. When I hug people, it won't feel like bricks. That is the superficial stuff. I am less than one percent likely to obtain breast cancer, down from 85 percent. I still await the sale of my home; we've relocated and started new jobs, but God is still in control. I am healing, preparing for the next surgery, and thankful and grateful that it is already worked out. I am just walking in what is already prepared for me. My spirit has never wavered. I have had peace and joy throughout this process. Despite the pain, I am thankful for the opportunity to prevent disease.

When I think of other people who may be faced with my decision, I can only pray they have the comfort and peace that God gave me. I always thought first about what really mattered to me.

The most important things on this Earth are my family and my life. Nothing that has to do with my physical body. I thanked God, and light heartedly blamed myself for putting this out into the atmosphere. I truly believe what you focus on, you bring to you; and in my youth, I was obsessed with the fact that I didn't have a real girl's body. Well, now I do, so I brought it on myself. For anyone faced with this, I hope you first know, as women, we are not defined by our bodies. With or without breasts, we are still sisters, moms, daughters, wives, and best friends to someone who loves us in all our imperfections. We also serve a God who is merciful; and even in your darkest hour, he sends angels to walk with you to help and encourage you. He knows just how much you can bear. There is pain, but it is not unbearable. The hardest thing to learn is that sometimes, you don't get from others what you give. Know that in life, you do for others what is in your heart; not so that you will get something back in return. Even if it's not from who you want it from, God will provide someone in place right on time. Find the joy in each day of your struggle. Your low is someone else's high, and your joy in your storm can be an encouragement to someone else. I am thankful for this journey, thankful I had choices my mom didn't, and thankful to be able to tell others how great my God is. Even when you should be afraid, He can take it away and give you a peace that doesn't make any sense and can only be The I AM.

Testimony of
Wesley and Karen Hilman
New Jersey
God Is Sovereign

My brethren, count it all joy when you fall into various trials, knowing that the testing of your faith produces patience. But let patience have its perfect work, that you may be perfect and complete, lacking nothing.

James 1: 2-4

Wes:

Now, if you're anything like me, you might be asking yourself: Why is it that when adversity strikes, one believer handles it well? He shines in and through adversity. He glorifies the Lord during his trial, while another believer will face a trial and not fare as well. What makes one believer better able to face adversity then another? And how can each of us learn to face adversity in a God-glorifying way?

These are some of the questions that brother James helps us to answer as he encourages fellow believers who are facing adversity. James is addressing the kind of adversity a person experiences when the believing is hard and pretending just doesn't work!

The Bible clearly teaches that every believer will experience some measure of trouble at different points in their lives. And although we may not like to think about it, God has not promised us a carefree life. The book of Job states: "For man is born of trouble as sparks fly upward. And man, who is born of woman, is short-lived and full of turmoil." (Job 5: 7, 14: 1)

Life's trials come from many different sources. In the final analysis, it really doesn't matter what the source of your trial stems from, because Jesus said: In this world you will have tribulation (trouble, tests)! (James 16: 33). It is within this framework that James writes these three verses and unpacks a fundamental truth of our Christian experience. That truth is that trials are a test of our faith. James starts out by saying: "My brethren, count it all joy when you fall into various trials. Now I must admit, my initial tendency is to skip over these words, especially the part about counting it all joy! You see, James commands us that regardless of the source of the trial, we are to have joy during it. He says to count it all joy, which is to consider it as, or to chalk it up to be, all joy when (not if) tests and trials come our way.

Oh really? I mean, right about now I'd like to raise my hand and nominate James 1:2 as one of the most outrageous verses in the Bible! How can James expect me to experience troubles and consider it all joy?

I don't know about you, but when I'm hurting, I want relief. When I hurt, I might get a little testy. When I hurt, I want to be waited on and pampered, and be the center of my wife Karen's attention. When I hurt, all I want to do is get in my bed, pull the covers up over my head, go into my manly-man bed cave and make the world go away! But count it all joy? I don't think so!

As if that weren't enough, the word James uses for joy means: to have pure, unmixed, unbridled, complete, and total joy. Now, that just about takes it over the top for me! James continues in verse two and says we should have this joy when we fall into various trials. The word he uses for various means trials of many different flavors. Trials that are complex and intricate. Trials that are diverse and variegated, which means trials of many colors, hews, and shades. It's the same word used to describe Joseph's many-colored coat.

James also indicates that since we don't fall into these trials by choice, we really can't prevent or avoid them.

These are trials we fall into when we least expect it. They often come as a surprise to us. This falling into is the same phrase used to describe what happened to the man the Good Samaritan helped. The man had unexpectedly fallen into trouble (Luke 10:30). James says: my brethren, count it all joy when you fall into various trials. But having said all of that, I must confess to you, I'm still a work in progress, because when I go back to the text and hear James say: My brethren, count it all joy; that is, chalk it up as pure, unmixed, unbridled, complete, and total joy when you fall into various trials. It can still be a hard pill to swallow!

Therefore, I decided to look at the text in some other translations to see if I might make better sense of it. Perhaps something was lost in my trustee old King James Version, with all its thees and thous.

Here's what I found:

The NIV says, Consider it pure joy.

The AMP states, Consider it wholly joy.

Wuest's translation says, Consider it a matter for unadulterated joy.

Hmm, not exactly what I was hoping to hear.

I got to thinking, maybe one of the paraphrased translations would be better.

The BBE version (The Bible in Basic English!) put it this way: let it be joy to you.

I then went to The Message, and it said: consider it a sheer gift, friends, when tests and challenges come at you from all sides.

So finally, I decided to read it in the Phillips paraphrase, which says: when trials come don't resent them as intruders, but welcome them as friends.

Thank you, Mr. Phillips, that was a tremendous help!

Which brings me full circle and at the risk of overstating the obvious. No matter how uncomfortable it may make me feel, there simply is no getting around it. Regardless of whether I like it or not, James say: My brethren, count it all joy when you fall into various trials.

At first glance, it almost seems as if, when faced with trouble, brother James is encouraging believers, to adopt Bobby McFerrin's song, Don't Worry Be Happy, as some sort of National Christian Anthem. If you know the words feel free to sing along with me:

Here's a little song I wrote . . .

You might want to sing it note-for-note:

Don't worry, be happy.

In every life, we have some trouble,

But when you worry, you make it double.

Don't worry, be happy now, be happy you all ...

But rest assured, this is not what James is saying. James is not calling Christians to be foolishly, blindly, and optimistically happy. James is also not saying to count pain and sorrow as good things in and of themselves. He certainly is not telling Christians to adopt a superficial gaiety in the face of life's adversities. In fact, James is not even encouraging us to be happy during trials, because there is a difference between joy and happiness. Happiness is based on happenstance or the events that befall us. In other words, if everything is ok, I'm happy; if not, I'm sad. As we all know, circumstances change.

I once heard someone say: Last night I went to bed feeling like I was on top of the world, but today I woke up feeling like the world was on top of me! Therefore, happiness is event centered. Brothers and sisters, joy is God centered. Consequently, the joy James calls us to embrace is supernatural. God's joy is a joy that goes against our human nature. Our natural response to trials is to get anxious and look for the first exit door. However, the joy James is referring to is God given! It is the second fruit of the spirit mentioned in Galatians 5: 22. When we decide to trust in what God says: He will give us joy even in the midst of our difficulties; James has in mind one of those days when the totally unexpected happens to us. One of those days when the events turn our world upside down. One of those days when a phone call, or a knock on the door, or a letter, or a meeting at work, or a doctor's report, sucks the air right out of our lungs!

One writer calls these incidences divinely disruptive moments. I am learning that it doesn't matter what you call them. They are moments which throw your mind into spin control as you search and try to figure out which way is up! Ultimately, moments like these have the potential to make us either spiritually better or spiritually bitter! It's kind of like the moment my wife, Karen, and I experienced some 10 years ago, when I developed a very persistent sinus headache. I had suffered with these headaches, off and on, over the course of 20 years. Therefore, as far as we were concerned, it was really no big thing. However, it is important to note that while Karen and I experienced the same event, it was from two different perspectives. So why don't I step aside and allow Karen to share her reflections first?

Karen:

Where shall I begin? Let me begin with what I can recall. I vividly recall God with us as He promised He would be. What a horrifying thought for me that I might lose my beloved, or that my beloved might lose his eyesight, or that he might lose the functioning of any part of his body that the brain, specifically the pituitary gland, might control. The trial came out of nowhere, or so I thought. To think, one week before Thanksgiving, which is Wes' favorite holiday. As I prayed fervently, I was reminded that the Lord is always preparing us for a time such as this; a trial. Just like the ever-loving, all-knowing Father that He is. He knows what is ahead of us, down the road, around the corner, at the top of the hill, perhaps.

Our preparation for all situations is to practice His presence! To practice that truth and all other truths is to believe what He has told us in His word. He will never leave us nor forsake us (Hebrew 13:5b). And He has promised to always be with us even to the end of the age (Matthew 28:20b). Even to the end of whatever trial we may be facing.

Our trial began with Wes experiencing what we thought was a sinus infection. My husband is prone to these infections, so we didn't think too much of this one until the headache symptoms persisted. I suggested that we go to the doctor's office instead of riding this one out. But my husband is the son of a nurse, so he thinks that this somehow qualifies him to prescribe treatments for his illnesses. Initially, he refused to go, but he finally relented. After the visit to the doctor, Wes' condition only worsened!

I remember standing in our bedroom with Wes as he complained about his vision. His head was now screaming pain, pain, and more pain. I don't remember whose decision it was for me to drive him to the emergency room instead of calling an ambulance. But that's what we did. As I tried to help him down the stairs from our second-floor bedroom, I realized with every step he took, the pain was like a violent blow to his head.

After what seemed to be forever, we finally arrived at the bottom of the steps. The trip from one floor to the next took a lot out of him. Wes had to rest before we attempted our trek to the car. It was clear to me that my beloved was in severe distress. I had never seen him like that before. My husband is 6'5", strong, and until this point appeared to be the picture of good health. It was very difficult to see him struggle with so much pain. I was scared. I prayed. I cautiously got him into the car, strapped him in, and off we flew on all four wheels to the hospital. Full speed ahead meant Wes felt every bump I hit and every curve I turned. His head continued to scream pain, pain, and more pain. I didn't mean to cause my beloved anymore pain than need be. I was just trying to get him to the hospital as quickly as possible. I was scared. I prayed.

We arrived at the hospital, and the doctors discovered that Wes had a brain tumor. And while I will allow Wes to share many of the details of what the doctors discovered, that disclosure lead to his being transferred to a regional hospital more equipped to deal with his diagnosis. They immediately rushed Wes by ambulance to this well-known trauma center in the area. I followed along in my car wondering, Lord, what exactly does all this mean? But the Lord had already begun to answer that question during the previous 24 hours by sending two good friends of ours to the local hospital. They prayed with us. One of the brothers stayed with me late into the night until it was time to transport Wes to our next destination. Their presence provided a level of comfort that directed me to give thanks to the Lord for always knowing what we need and when we need it.

We got to the regional hospital and went through the usual, who are you and how are you paying. As God would have it, Wes did not have to wait for a room. Whenever Wes and I are made aware of a hospital stay of someone we know, we ask the Lord to allow at least one Christian to be a part of the care team. It could be anyone who may touch that patient, from the attending physician to a custodian praying as he or she empties the trash. This hospital stay was no different.

We no sooner made our request when a nurse technician came into the room who was a believer. Shortly thereafter, a nurse practitioner popped into the room. The glory of the Lord was projected as soon as she entered. She asked Wes several questions, and during the conversation, it became apparent that we all belonged to Him. She then initiated prayer. We held hands, and that sister took us to the throne room! The Lord was making His presence known! I felt He was saying: let there be no doubt in your mind. I'm here. I will not leave you alone.

After that, doctors came and went. Nurses came and went. Patient care technicians came and went. Members of the medical team were drawing Wes' blood, taking his temperature, checking his vitals. After sending Wes for an MRI, it was determined that he should have surgery the very next morning to remove the tumor. They feared if they didn't operate, Wes would lose his eyesight. Brain surgery! Really, Lord? I was scared. I prayed. How quickly we forget. How fickle our flesh is. The Lord had just assured me that He was in this, and that He would not leave us alone. So, no matter what this looked like, and it didn't look good, He is present. It is reassuring to know the truth and to believe it. The truth does set you free from fearing the unknown. I didn't know how any of this was going to turn out. When practicing His presence, I did know He promised to be with me even to the end of the age.

I spent the night with my beloved; not wanting to leave him, I slept in a recliner. I did sleep for the most part. Early the next morning, I decided to run home, shower, change, and check on my mom, who lives with us. I needed to get back in time to be with Wes before they wheeled him down to the operating room for his scheduled surgery. I returned to his room to find him still there, with a rather perplexed look on his face. But I'll let Wes share why he appeared to have that look.

As family and friends became aware of Wes' condition, they began to visit. The look of concern on their faces as each one entered his hospital room led us to believe that they only had part of the story. The part where they heard Wes has a brain tumor. We, of course, were thrilled to be able to tell them the rest of the story. A praise party ensued. We held hands with half a dozen folks and worshipped our Lord. We sang and gave thanks through prayer. Medical staff and visitors passed by the room. You could tell from their facial expressions, they were baffled. One of the Christian brothers from the medical staff who had prayed with us before passing by the room; he joined us. And to Wes' unbelieving roommate, none of this went unnoticed. But I'll let Wes share that part of the story.

I only know what His word tells me, and how I experience His truth through the life He has given me by practicing His presence: Yours, O Lord, is the greatness and the power and the glory and the victory and the majesty... and You rule over all, and in Your hand is power and might; and it lies in Your hand to make great and to strengthen everyone. (1 Chronicles 29: 11-12). Having shared some of what I was feeling, let me turn the rest of the story back to Wes.

Wes:

Well, the first thing I would have you know is before I ended up at the doctor's office and eventually the hospital, I was also earnestly praying that the Lord would take away the headache. However, it seemed like the more I prayed, the more intense the sinus headache became. So, I went into confessional mode, and I confessed everything I could think of. When that didn't work, I confessed some sins I had invented on behalf of my great grandfather (whom I never met)! But still to no avail, the headache persisted. I started wrestling with God: You've healed these headaches before; why won't you do so now? You heal others, and I'm your son, so why won't you take my headache away?

The more I prayed, the more it seemed like my prayers were rising to the ceiling and falling back to the floor!

As Karen has already mentioned, she insisted, against my insistence I must add, that we go to the doctor's. To my shame, I broke the unwritten manly-man code and gave in. Well the doctor saw me, gave me an antibiotic and some extra strength Tylenol and sent me home. But I still got no relief. The headache pain only intensified!

The next day we went to the emergency room. The doctor decided to do something that hadn't been done for me in the past. He ordered a CAT scan to determine which sinuses were causing me so much discomfort. A few minutes after the CAT scan, the doctor came in and said: Mr. Hillman, you're right, you do have a sinus infection, but that's not your real problem. You have a tumor, a mass, a growth, the size of a golf ball surrounding your pituitary gland! Since we're not equipped to deal with this type of thing, we're going to immediately transfer you to a regional medical hospital where they will probably schedule emergency surgery for you tomorrow morning!"

Now I'd like to say that my immediate response was: Praise the Lord, count it all for joy, which was followed by a recitation of familiar Bible verses. You know ones, like: The Lord is a stronghold in the day of trouble; or I will hide in the shadow of your wings until this danger has passed; or God is our refuge and strength, a very present help in trouble. Therefore, we will not fear (Nahum 1:7; Psalm 57: 1; Psalm 46: 1-2a). But the truth be told, being the spiritual giant that I am, all I wanted to do was take my 6'5" frame, find a corner, stick my thumb in my mouth, and curl up in the fetal position.

My first, second, and probably third reaction was not to count it all as joy. I mean, all I could think of was: You gotta be kidding me! You got the wrong person, or the wrong CAT scan or both! The fact is, the doctor's news rocked me to the bottom of my hospital booties! I couldn't believe what I was hearing.

For me, this is exactly the type of trial that James is talking about. A trial that is unexpected, and humanly speaking, unwanted and uninvited. A trial that I had fallen into which caught me completely by surprise! But you see, the Lord in His infinite wisdom, knew. He knew that if He answered my prayers and removed my sinus headache, the tumor would have gone undetected. The tumor had grown and developed over the course of a decade or so and was the consistency of quartz with many jagged edges. It had already begun to engulf my carotid artery and left optic nerve. Therefore, if the tumor had continued to grow undetected, it could have severed either of those vessels and led to blindness or possibly even a stroke. As it was, the tumor had already begun to affect the sight in my left eye. I noticed this because directly across the wall from my hospital bed was a chalkboard that the hospital staff used to write the names of the attending physician and the nurse assigned to my room, along with various medical information. I had my glasses on and tried to read the words on the chalkboard. But much to my dismay it was blurry, and I really had to squint just to discern a few of the letters.

And then the questions began. You know, all the questions that begin with the three-letter word: WHY? Why me Lord? Why not someone else? Why not someone who doesn't love you, and who doesn't want to serve you? Why this, Lord? Why now? Why not later? Why not much later, like sometime after the rapture? Even during all my "why me" questions, God was at work assuring us that He was in control! We discovered one of the ways that He did this was through believers on staff at the hospital.

One of the first people we met when we got to the hospital room was a patient care technician. We got to talking, and he let me know that he was a Christian and said he would be praying for me. The next person to come into the room was a nurse practitioner, and the same thing happened. The nurse practitioner let us know she was a believer. She then asked if we would like her to pray for me. As she did, the patient care technician must've been passing by the room because he heard her praying, came in and joined us!

God has a way of letting us know that we are not alone! He can flood our souls with His presence, as well as bring us comfort by surrounding us with our brothers and sisters in Christ Jesus! On the morning of the surgery, which was scheduled for nine; Karen, who spent the night with me at the hospital, left around six to go home and check on her mother. She couldn't have been gone for more than 10 minutes when the physician, who was the head of the surgical team, came in to see me.

As I look back on it, I know that it was the Lord's providence that Karen left when she did, because she is a prayer warrior and a woman who has the gift of faith. I, on the other hand, am neither of those things. God clearly wanted me to be alone to test and grow my faith and dependence on Him. Much to my surprise, the surgeon said he thought there might be a different direction we could go instead of surgery. He also said he had to sell the rest of the surgical team on his idea. His thought was to treat the tumor medicinally with a medication around since the 1920s, and somewhat successful in abating the growth of pituitary tumors.

Imagine! This was a physician who makes his living by performing operations, who was now suggesting a nonsurgical solution, after saying that surgery was immediate and imperative. His change of direction should not have come as a surprise to me, because God is the one who turns hearts and minds in the direction He wants them to go! However, before he left, and before I had the opportunity to skip merrily out of the hospital, the doctor added that he had to go to the surgical team and explain his idea. He wanted me to be clear that if any one of them raised their hand in disagreement, the surgery would go forward as scheduled!

The the operating physician went on to his mission. I turned to the Word. In times of trouble there are certain scriptures I will read and meditate on, like Jeremiah 29:11: For I know the plans I have for you, plans for good and not for evil, to give you a future and a hope. So, I got my Bible and tried to turn to Jeremiah 29:11 as quickly as possible. I flicked through the pages to get to my destination as fast as I could. My first flick took me to Ezekiel. I flicked the pages again, and the page heading said Jeremiah 30:14. Therefore, I knew I only had to turn back one more page before I would be where I wanted to be.

Before I could turn the page, something strangely supernatural happened! To my shock, the page grayed out and one verse, Jeremiah 30:17, was elevated off the page!

Now remember, as I mentioned before, I had noticed a subtle diminution of my sight, as evidenced by when I tried to read the chalkboard in my room. I attributed the verse's elevated appearance to my afflicted eyesight. So, I turned away from the Bible and looked across the room for a moment, thinking I needed to refocus my eyes. When I looked back at my Bible, the verse was still suspended about a half foot above the page. It almost looked like a hologram, except the letters from the verse were an emboldened black. It was as if the verse was undergirded by some sort of invisible scaffolding.

My wife, Karen, is the prayer warrior and faith walker in our family. So, it hadn't dawned on me yet that the Lord was trying to get my attention! I continued to think that I needed to refocus my eyes, rather than simply read the verse. This time, I closed my eyes and squinted tightly. When I reopened them, the result was the same! The verse was still suspended and the rest of the page was still grayed out. By this time, you probably have surmised that I'm not the brightest light bulb on the porch. The thought finally dawned on me: Read the verse dumb-dumb! I proceeded to read, and it said: For

I will restore you to health. And I will heal you of your wounds, declares the Lord (Jeremiah 30:17). I read it again, and a sense of peace began to pervade my soul. God was at work!

Again, I must confess I'm not a spiritual giant whose faith can move mountains. You see, I'm still trying to learn, day by day, how the Lord works in my life, day by day, for it is in Him that we live and move and have our being; and our times are in His hands! (Acts 17: 28, Psalm 31: 15).

Unfortunately, I immediately proceeded to interrupt the peace the Lord was trying to pour into my soul by going into my theological analysis mode. You need to know that I'm not a big name it and claim it or blab it and grab it kind of guy. I began to reason with God: I know that you're going to heal me, Lord, for you promised that in heaven there will be no more pain or suffering, which means there certainly aren't going to be any more diseases to afflict us. So, I guess you are telling me you're going to take me home and heal me, then and there. Because you couldn't possibly be telling me that you're going to heal me in the here and now. As I reread the verse and pondered it, the Lord impressed upon my heart that He was going to heal and preserve me now.

Well, after while the physician came back and said the team had agreed to try treating the tumor medicinally. As Karen would share with me later, this should not have been a surprise, because the Lord is the one who touches the hearts and minds of men and bends them to be in accordance with His will: For from Him and through Him and to Him are all things. To Him be the glory forever. Amen (Romans 11:36).

However, before leaving, the doctor added one very important caveat. The medicine he was suggesting was supposed to abate the growth of the tumor over time. He quickly added that in the short term (meaning over the next 24 hours), it should also help to improve my eyesight. The doctor made it clear that if this did not occur, the surgery would be back on the table and rescheduled for the following morning. With that the doctor left, and wouldn't you know it Karen reappears! So, once again it was evident that God wanted me to be alone with Him so that I could experience His presence in a new way.

I proceeded to tell Karen all that had occurred in her absence. What struck me most was that she did not marvel over, or dwell on the elevated verse the way I had. Whereas, I initially thought it was my physical eyes deceiving me, Karen simply accepted what happened through the eyes of faith! In fact, she had more questions about what the doctor said pertaining to the medicine then she did about the miraculously elevated verse.

In the meantime, the clock was ticking on the doctor's mandate. There must be immediate improvement in my eyesight, or else the surgery was back on for the following morning. No problem for God!

A few hours passed, and I was drowsily taking a nap. When I awoke (without putting on my glasses), I glanced across the room, and to my surprise, I could read all the information on the chalkboard! Mind you, as I mentioned, I was unable to read it before, even with my glasses on! Here's the miraculous part. All of this occurred before I received a single dose of the medication the doctor had prescribed!

When the nurse came in to give me the first dosage of the medicine, I read the chart for her without my glasses. The nurse was astounded and called the attending physician, who thought there must've been a mistake, and that I must had already received a dosage of the medication; the mention of it must have been mistakenly omitted from my chart. The nurse stood her ground and said that no such thing had occurred! The physician then ordered an eye specialist to visit me that evening to perform some tests to determine if, in fact, my sight had improved. All the tests indicated it had! Karen let me know that this was yet another sign that God was truly in control, because the question had to be asked: what was the tumor responding to? As she said, the answer was supernaturally obvious. The tumor was responding to the healing hand of our ever-present Father!

In case you might be wondering, the Lord has continued to restore my health. Until this past year, I had to visit the hospital twice a year to have MRIs of my pituitary gland. Six months after my hospital stay, an MRI was taken. It revealed the tumor had gone from crystalline to the consistency of oatmeal; drastically reducing the possibility of severing either the carotid artery or optic nerve! Within a year, the growth of the tumor was not only abated, but the size of it had begun to diminish, relinquishing its vice grip on my carotid artery and optic nerve. Subsequent visits attest to the fact that it continues to slowly shrink in size. During our last visit, the doctor mentioned that if this progress continues, the dosage of the medicine might be even be reduced!

However, God's purpose and perspective always

goes way beyond our immediate needs and stretches into eternity. Yes, He certainly did and continues to take care of me: For the mercy and love of the Lord is from everlasting to everlasting on those who fear Him, and His righteousness with their children's children. (Ps 103: 17). Although the focus of our prayers, along with five churches, was for my healing, God was at work on a completely different level! When I initially got to the hospital, I was in the room by myself. On the second day, another patient was brought into the room. As we had conversation about why we were there, he shared with me that he had real health challenges, as well.

He clearly was watching and listening as believers came to visit me. I'm sure he overheard some of the prayers sent up around us. As the Lord would have it, I got to share the Gospel with him before he went home. He accepted the Lord Jesus Christ as his Savior! Little did I know his family had been praying for his salvation as well. God is always working in ways that we can't begin to fathom!

God is always on time. He doesn't arrive a minute too early or a minute too late. He comes when He, and He alone, can receive all the glory for what He brings to pass in each of our lives. Humanly speaking, I was glad to be going home to spend Thanksgiving with my family and give thanks for a new brother in Christ. Again, to God be the Glory! Having said all of that, I must confess to you, I'm still a work in progress, because when I go back to James 1: 2 and read: My brethren, count it all joy (that is chalk it up as pure, unmixed, unbridled, complete, and total joy when you fall into various trials); it can still be a hard pill to swallow! But James doesn't leave us there, because in verses three and four he says: knowing that the testing of your faith produces patience. But let patience have its perfect work, that you may be perfect and complete, lacking nothing.

Now the English language does not do justice to the word James chose to use for patience or endurance. The kind of patience James has in mind means to stay and be steadfast while under the pressure of the trial. It means, hold your ground rather than looking for a way to escape, no matter how long the trial lasts! Here's the wonderful part. The word James chose for patience and endurance is always also connected with hope! It is not so much the patience borne of grinning and gritting your teeth as you resolutely lean into a hurricane. It refers more to the patience you exercise while waiting for someone. James is saying that while we are standing steadfastly under the pressure of the trial, we can do so because we are expectantly waiting for someone to come along and help us, and therefore we have hope! Our great hope and expectation during our times of trial, as we wait for our change to come, is that Jesus will arrive and see us through the trial! As I consider this, the truth of Hebrews 10: 23 and 12:2a come into clearer focus: Let us hold fast to the confession of our hope without wavering for He who promised is faithful ... Looking to Jesus the author and finisher of our faith. As we wait, these are the moments when God stretches and cultivates our faith. These are the moments when we discover the depths of His love for us. These are the moments when we find out that the Lord truly is a stronghold in our day of trouble.

These are the moments when we learn the truth, if God be for us, who (or what) can be against us. These are the moments in which we more fully understand that we are truly God's children, and He is our Father, our Abba, our Daddy!

Now after James has encouraged us to wait patiently and hope for the Lord, he could have stopped and moved on to something else. There is one more nugget he has for us to mine. The word patience or endurance also carries the connotation of hardening. Therefore, as

God helps us to be steadfast under the trial, He is also in the process of making our patience more durable. This is why in verse three James says: But let patience have its perfect work, that you may be perfect and complete, lacking nothing. James says that the testing of our faith perfects and matures it so that we are better equipped to handle additional trials as we learn to trust God more and more. Through it all I'm also learning to ask better questions. Questions that begin with the word, WHAT rather then WHY. What Lord? What would you have me to learn? What are you trying to teach me about you? What are you trying to teach me about myself? What would you have me to do?

And so, my brothers and sisters, if you're having a difficult time rejoicing in your times of suffering, just keep reminding yourself this is not how the story ends. Jesus will show up to help us through our trials now. We need to also have and keep an eternal focus, because what we experience now is not the concluding chapter. It's simply the rough side of the mountain that leads to our heavenly home, where the best is yet to come!

So, let's end where we began: Therefore, my brothers and sisters, consider it pure joy, whenever you fall into trials of many kinds, because you know that the testing of your faith develops perseverance. But let patience have its perfect work, that you may be perfect and complete, lacking nothing.

To God be the Glory!

Rev. Eugene L. Neville

R ev. Eugene L. Neville was born and raised in the city of Boston, Massachusetts. He received his bachelors of arts from Barrington College, and his masters of divinity from Gordon-Conwell Theological Seminary. He did post graduate studies at several universities in the New England. For 10 years, he served at the Historic Twelfth Baptist Church in Roxbury, under the pastorate of Rev. Dr. Michael E. Haynes. In 1981, he became the Founder and Pastor of the Mount Moriah Baptist Church, Inc. in the city of Brockton, Massachusetts.

After serving with distinction in the Christian

ministry for over 45 years, he is retired. Before retiring, he had developed and implemented numerous mentoring and social outreach ministries, not only for the benefit of his congregates, but for the broader community. Simultaneously, he served others in the city of Boston. He was the first project director of the Black Church Capacity Building Program for a leading philanthropic foundation; a program which provided substantial grants to assist churches in their social outreach ministries. In addition, Rev. Neville was one of the founding members of the Center for Urban Ministerial Education in Boston, an urban extension of Gordon-Conwell Theological Seminary, providing classes and training which prepare men and women for greater support ministries within an urban context.

While serving in his capacity as the pastor of the Mount Moriah Baptist Church, Inc., Rev. Neville further served on a variety of boards within the greater Brockton community. He left the city with a rich legacy through the establishment of the Amara Computer Learning Center, Inc., The Emergency Food and Home Goods Distribution Program for the homeless and needy. He also developed the first video-conferencing Prison Family Reunification Ministry, utilizing technology as a resource to help reintegrate former inmates back into their families, work force, and community. He assisted many churches around the country, helping them acquire video-conferencing equipment, training, and computer ministry templates that could be useful in social settings. In partnership with a national philanthropic institution, he developed the Brockton Higher Education Research Center, a program designed to assist socially and economically marginalized youth prepare for and gain entrance into college.

Rev. Neville has counseled many people through life-altering experiences. He helped people find balance in their life, and also taught them how to achieve their goal for excellence. He mentored many men and woman who desire to enhance their spiritual gift and skill sets, and better understand their divine assignments for such times as these.

Rev. Neville is a man with a vision, a commitment to encourage and empower people to live above their human constrictions, and to strive toward emotional balance, excellence, and spiritual healing. He is the author of The Corridors of Strange Darkness, Struggling with Glaucoma. He is also the author of three books which will soon be published: God's Corridors of Healing, I

Stand Amazed, Inspirational Thoughts, and Profiles of Faith and Praise.

Rev. Neville and his wife Ruth are the proud parents of two adult daughters, five grandchildren, and one great granddaughter.

Made in the USA
Lexington, KY
17 November 2019